Zephyr Press

3316 N. Chapel Avenue
P.O. Box 66006
Tucson, AZ 85728-6006
(602) 322-5090
FAX (602) 323-9402

WHAT NEXT?

WHAT NEXT?

Futuristic Scenarios for Creative Problem Solving

Robert E. Myers and E. Paul Torrance

Zephyr Press
Tucson, Arizona

What Next?
Futuristic Scenarios for Creative Problem Solving

For teachers of grades 6–12

Printed in the United States of America

ISBN 1-56976-001-2

Editors: Stacey Lynn and Stacey Shropshire
Cover design: David Fischer
Design and production: Nancy Taylor
Typesetting: Alphagraphics

Zephyr Press
P.O. Box 66006
Tucson, Arizona 85728-6006

Library of Congress Cataloging-in-Publication Data
Myers, Robert E., 1924-
What next? : futuristic scenarios for creative problem solving / Robert E. Myers and E. Paul Torrance.
p. cm.
Includes bibliographical references.
ISBN 1-56976-001-2 (alk. paper)
1. Creative thinking–Study and teaching. 2. Decision-making--Study and teaching. 3. English language–Composition and exercises–Study and teaching. I. Torrance, E. Paul (Ellis Paul), 1915- . II. Title.
LB1590.5.M94 1994 94-3990
370. 15'2–dc20 CIP

Tell all the truth but tell it slant.
Success in circuit lies,
Too bright for our infirm delight
The truth's superb surprise.

As lightning to the children eased
With explanation kind,
The truth must dazzle gradually
Or every man be blind.

—Emily Dickinson

Contents

Contents

Preface

We hope that *What Next?* provides you with a vehicle that will aid you in helping your students achieve at least three important goals:

- Improve their creative writing and communication skills.
- Improve their skills in creative problem solving.
- Enlarge, enrich, and make more accurate their images of the future.

Perhaps the most important and most basic skills that we can teach our students today are those involved in communication and creative problem solving. In fact, the teaching of these skills may really be the key to our students' successful learning of the other basic skills such as reading, writing, doing mathematics, understanding science, and the like.

Since communication skills have become ever more important as electronic technologies have emerged and developed in the twentieth century, it is imperative that young people master the fundamental skills of reading, writing, speaking, and listening in order to participate in the workings of our society in the twenty-first century. Moreover, by their efforts to solve real problems creatively, young people must develop those skills fully if they are to function effectively in their personal and vocational lives. Students are not motivated to master these skills and other basics unless they can see a connection between these basics and their future lives. Motivation requires some kind of "long look."

We know that today's students are motivated to learn about the future. In a number of studies, high school students rank studies of the future as the most important subject. There are good reasons for this ranking. Today's students will live as adults in a world vastly different from today's world. They will do kinds of work that do not exist today. The pace of change will probably require them to alter their work and associated lifestyle several times during their lives. This will require abilities and information that we cannot imagine today. However, we can be certain that these tasks will require creative problem solving and strong communication skills.

We believe that these important life skills can be developed through practice in creative writing. In *What Next?* we have provided material that we believe will help you motivate your students to do a variety of kinds of creative writing. We offer a number of suggestions to help you accomplish these tasks. We hope that you will not limit yourself to these ideas and that you will not try to use suggestions that do not fit your style of teaching.

Three or four levels of involvement are provided in each activity or unit. We believe that students can warm themselves up to good creative writing and communication by producing some ideas and then doing something with these ideas—letting one thing lead to another. "Creativity begets creativity!"

Regardless of how you use these materials, we hope that you will interact with your students about their experiences and talk with them about their thinking and whatever creative writing they produce. We would like to recommend for your consideration a procedure suggested by Edward de Bono (1974) for talking with people about their performance in a creative task. This procedure involves discussions with students in four areas: (1) praise, (2) clarification, (3) criticism, and (4) amplification.

PRAISE: Find something about the writing or ideas produced that you can honestly praise. If a student completes the exercise or responds to the invitation to write a poem, story, advertisement, or joke, this is an achievement worthy of praise. The student has faced a problem and come up with a solution or solutions.

CLARIFICATION: In a discussion, try to get the student to clarify some point in his or her writing or response to the problems posed by the exercise. It is definitely not a criticism area and should precede any criticism. Unless you understand what the student is trying to do, it is unfair to criticize the work. In this discussion, you should honestly try to understand what the student has done. Encourage the student to discuss what he or she has done. Once the matter has been clarified, that is enough.

CRITICISM: This is a difficult area of discussion for some teachers. You should not feel compelled to criticize, but if the need arises, the following simple rules may help:

1. Never criticize in a general way. Be specific. Criticize in terms of some specified criteria.
2. Lead the student gently to see for him- or herself what the weakness is. It is important that students learn to see mistakes for themselves, not just accept such information on authority.

AMPLIFICATION: This is an important area and should lead to further growth and encourage a kind of incubation that will cause learning to continue. Comments can be made to encourage the student to think further about his or her production. It may involve filling in gaps of some kind. It may open up something that has been hidden or glossed over. It may clarify the reasons that something happened. It may suggest other ways—better alternatives. It may establish a connection with the future.

Above all, let these materials and the use of them become a challenge to your own creativity.

Reference

de Bono, E. *Thinking Course for Juniors.* Blandford Forum, Dorset, England: Direct Education Services, 1974.

Robert E. Myers
Eugene, Oregon

E. Paul Torrance
Athens, Georgia

Introduction

To the Teacher

Preparing for the Units

There are very good reasons for our suggesting that you introduce the units and not simply assign them without any explanation. One basic reason for your leading in to the units is that you can determine what ideas might be appropriate for warming up and motivating your students so that they will be prepared to respond. You know best what ideas are suitable in spurring your students' thinking.

We perceive another important reason for your "setting up" the activities, namely, you could very well decide from your students' reactions that their mood will produce indifferent or negative results. If that is the case, it is usually a good procedure to switch to another activity. Master teachers are not afraid to throw out their original schedule and head in a different direction.

On the other hand, a teacher has to be a bit optimistic: some activities turn out very well when it seems as if they wouldn't. As you know, there are students who almost always complain when they are asked to write anything. Having a successful effort will usually cure them of this malady.

Success is crucial to *your* attitude also, and so, to begin with, you should select a unit that seems "surefire" (although there are certainly no guarantees of that in teaching). Find a unit in the book that seems especially suitable for your students, one that is also appropriate to your curricular objectives. Generally speaking, the units have something going for them; that is, they are usually a change from regular curricular offerings. That advantage, coupled with a little enthusiasm on your part (the necessary ingredient in any academic offering), won't ensure success, but success should be obtainable.

Torrance offers the following suggestions to teachers to help them warm up students for creative thinking:

- Question students to heighten expectation and anticipation.
- Create an awareness of a problem to be solved, a possible future need, or a difficulty to be faced.
- Heighten concern about a problem or future need.
- Stimulate curiosity and the desire to know.
- Make the strange familiar and the familiar strange.
- Free students' minds from inhibiting mind sets.
- Look at the same information from different viewpoints.
- Ask provocative questions to make the learner think of information in new ways.
- Predict from limited information.
- Show the connection between the expected learning and current problems or a future career.
- Provide only enough structure to give clues and direction.
- Use a physical warm-up activity that is related to the information to be presented.

Torrance goes on to say that "in using activities of the kinds listed above, the teacher must keep in mind the purposes of such experiences:

- to create the desire to know,
- to heighten anticipation and expectation,
- to get attention,
- to arouse curiosity,
- to tickle imagination, and
- to give purpose and motivation."

Predicting the Future

As you probably know, predicting future events has become a very popular activity in the past decade or so. People devote enormous amounts of energy to producing forecasts concerning every phase of human and infrahuman existence, from next year to more than a thousand years from now. Futurism is a pastime for some, a vocation for some, a cult and a way of life for others. These are some of the predictions learned people are making for the next several decades:

- A genetic science revolution
- A global antipollution crusade supported by all elements of society
- Loop cities combined with high-speed rail to create "super metro areas"
- Global communications with automatic language translation for almost everyone everywhere
- Implementation of a realistic global program for controlling population
- The use of solar energy in highly efficient systems for desalinizing seawater in very large volumes
- "Smart" cars and "smart" roads (with robot-run vehicles on designated routes)
- Domed cities and bubble farms
- A new generation of transatmospheric vehicles
- Hydrogen as a cost-competitive fuel
- A megacorporate global economy
- The mutations of HIV-1 into new species
- The linking of human brains to computers
- New biotechnological discoveries that help millions of people with disabilities
- Effective means of neutralizing old nuclear wastes
- Human-powered flight
- Rival companies offering inexpensive trips to the moon and space colonies supporting mining and tourism
- An asteroid warning/defense system (with batteries of huge missiles) to prevent disastrous collisions

Those who have thought deeply about the distant future foresee the following changes (among a great many being currently envisioned):

- The human species will radiate into many subspecies and subcultures that will become increasingly alien to each other.
- There will be a proliferation of new important religions.
- Selfhood and individuality will dissolve as progress is made toward the equivalent of telepathy and shared consciousness.

- More than once in the next few hundred years there will be substantial kill-offs of the human species because of conflict or technological carelessness.
- Within the next 5,000 years a swarm of asteroids will hit Earth.

Futurism is a fascinating topic and an engrossing way of thinking. In administering the units that follow, you may want to consult one of the many excellent publications devoted to looking at the future.

To the Student

Each of the activities in this book is designed to help you attain at least three important goals:

- Improve your creative writing and communication skills.
- Improve your creative problem-solving skills.
- Enlarge, enrich, and make more accurate your image of the future.

All of these are important skills you will be using the rest of your life.

You will live as an adult in a world vastly different from today's world. Most likely, you will do work of a kind that does not exist today. The pace of change will probably require that you alter your work and its associated lifestyle several times during your life. These alterations will require abilities, skills, and information that we cannot imagine today. The dangers of future shock are great. This shock can be avoided or lessened if you acquire an understanding of future problems and creative problem-solving skills for dealing with them.

In *What Next?* we invite you to explore a variety of aspects of the future through a variety of creative problem solving and writing. We hope that you will accept these invitations and find each exploration challenging, exciting, and rewarding.

1
What Next?

An Invitation to Write an Advertisement

Overview

The initial unit of this book deals with one of the most important activities of creative production—combining ideas and elements. The kind of combining in "What Next?" is the obvious kind in which a toaster is combined with an oven, or a knife sharpener is added to a can opener. In this unit, it is supposed that manufacturers of appliances, furniture, and vehicles will continue this combining trend in the future. The business of this unit is to involve your students in guessing what combinations are in store for us.

Creative Thinking Skill to Be Developed: Combining Ideas and Elements

This first unit attempts to involve your students in a basic and natural way of creating: putting things together. Children make believe that ordinary objects are cars, people, monsters, buildings, machines, and so on, when they play. They also quite naturally combine those objects in ways that make the objects into other imaginary things.

In the last three decades, retail merchandising has become almost obsessed with performing the same trick, combining two, three, and even more items into new products. The last time we glanced at a catalogue, this combining and recombining business was still in full swing. Undoubtedly the idea of putting together three or four appliances is "old hat" to your students, but the feat may have been done so often now as to present a challenge to them when it comes to combining in new ways those items we have listed in the unit.

Preparing for the Unit

It is a good idea to introduce an activity with something visible, audible, or tangible if it is possible to do so. In the event you happen to have the kind of watch advertised at the beginning of the student unit, you will have the perfect prop for introducing the unit. If you don't have that marvel of technology, any other portable gadget combining two or more functions will serve nearly as well.

Presenting the Unit

The unit begins with a genuine advertisement of watches that feature musical alarms, calculators, calendars, and "countdowns." The ad is not presented in its entirety, but the information is authentic. As we note in the unit, the prices will certainly change, but what is an ad without prices?

At the second level, the student is asked to combine three products and thereby "manufacture" a product of the future. He or she may choose from among more than forty common appliances, pieces of furniture, and entertainment devices. You may want to substitute other items for the ones listed in the four columns.

This task requires the kind of playful attitude that is conducive to genuine creative effort. If the student's thinking is irreverent, frivolous, or impractical, don't be too upset. We would discourage combinations in bad taste. (We've attempted to avoid some combinations that could prove embarrassing, but that kind of thinking is inevitable in some individuals.) The student will have to write an advertisement for his or her creation, and so there may be considerable rethinking done at the next stage.

The Writing Assignment

There are two tasks for the student to perform if he or she accepts the invitation to write an advertisement for the new product. First, a decision has to be made as to which medium would be the most appropriate for advertising the product. Second, the student must compose the ad. Perhaps you can be of considerable help in this part of the unit. You can present the principles of good advertising to your class so that students can compose ads intelligently. Although the whole activity is based upon imaginative speculation, encourage your students to write attractive, persuasive ads.

References

Barzun, Jacques. *Simple and Direct: A Rhetoric for Writers.* New York: Harper & Row, 1975.

Mitchell, Richard. *Less than Words Can Say.* Boston: Little, Brown, 1979.

Zinsser, William. *On Writing Well.* 2d ed. New York: Harper & Row, 1980.

1 What Next?

1. Here are the highlights of a recent newspaper advertisement. (The prices will undoubtedly have changed by the time you read this.)

FANTASTIC WATCH SALE!

- Water Sports Casio—water resistant, date (calendar), countdown, daily and hourly alarm . . . **$29.88**
- Alarm Chronograph—stopwatch, daily and hourly alarm . . . **$24.88**
- 2-Way Casio—analog and digital, calendar, stopwatch, melody alarm. . . **$49.95**
- Calculator Chronograph—hour, date, day; 8-digit 4-function; alarms; stopwatch; varied tones . . . **$54.88**
- Musical Alarm—variety of date, alarm melodies; countdown and stopwatch . . . **$17.88**

Not only can we buy a wristwatch with a musical alarm clock, a calendar, and a calculator, but we can purchase a television set that is also a telephone. Manufacturers have been combining such a great variety of appliances and gadgets to make life easier and more entertaining for us that more and more of these combinations can be expected in the years to come. Sometimes, though, someone gets carried away. Once, before the advent of transistors, a manufacturer of ranges tried to entertain the cook by adding a radio to the appliance—with predictable results. After the first chicken was roasted, the condensers melted and the householder had to turn on another radio or the TV if she or he wanted to be entertained while cooking.

What Next? *(continued)*

2. In the future, there is sure to be more combining of things that we have become accustomed to. Which three of the items listed below might possibly be combined into a new, irresistible product? You can make up your "new" product from among this list of potential components:

chair	**broom**	**trumpet**	**camera**
compass	**computer terminal**	**guitar**	**smoke detector**
hat	**bicycle**	**bathtub**	**walkie-talkie**
television set	**telephone**	**car**	**bed**
fishing pole	**table**	**saw**	**vacuum cleaner**
lamp	**desk**	**thermometer**	**lawn mower**
cup	**pen**	**pickup truck**	**fireplace**
watch	**knife**	**mirror**	**piano**
pencil	**knife sharpener**	**toothbrush**	**toaster**
pencil sharpener	**scooter**	**freezer**	**refrigerator**
skillet	**sewing machine**	**skis**	

Item 1 ____________________

Item 2 ____________________

Item 3 ____________________

What Next? *(continued)*

Describe this future product. If you'd like, draw a picture or diagram of it.

What Next? *(continued)*

3. Now that you have your new product designed, how would you advertise it? What medium—newspaper, billboard, magazine, television, or radio—would be best suited to proclaim its advantages to the public?

Why is the medium you chose the best for your advertisement?

You can sketch out your ideas for advertising in this medium in the space below.

2
Blessings in Disguise

An Invitation to Write a Short Story

Overview

The unit consists of an introduction about the idea that what may appear to be very unfortunate can turn out quite well for us. Then your students are asked to explain how thirteen apparently negative happenings could turn into blessings. Finally, your students are invited to construct a plot for a short story around some blessing in disguise.

Creative Thinking Skills to Be Developed: Looking from a Different Perspective; Being Original

Torrance (1979; Torrance and Safter 1990) has made "Looking at It a Different Way" one of eighteen creative thinking skills that can be developed in young people in the classroom. It is an extremely important skill for all kinds of people—scientists, architects, artists, engineers, mathematicians, and a host of others. Of the eighteen skills, it, along with "Being Original," is the most fun for people who are a bit different from others by nature—a little off kilter. You may have one or two students in your class who fall into that category.

You should encourage your students before writing their short stories to follow their own ideas and not be unduly influenced by the plots of the television programs, movies, and books with which they are acquainted. Of course, it is impossible not to be influenced in some way by tales writers have produced and to which we have been exposed, but your students can rely largely on their own experiences and ideas in writing their short stories.

Preparing for the Unit

Since blessings in disguise occur fairly frequently (the optimists among us probably can find more of them than the so-called realists), you just might have a good example of one for leading into this unit. In addition to the thirteen listed at the second level of the unit, a great many blessings in disguise could possibly have happened to you in your teaching career. To illustrate, has one or more of these "disasters" happened to you and then turned out to be a blessing?

- Being transferred to another school that you thought was one in which you'd never want to teach.
- Getting your assignment changed at the last minute so that you were teaching a course you hadn't taught before (and didn't want to teach).
- Finding a student in class with a reputation that made you want to have him or her in anyone's class but yours.
- Getting laryngitis just before Christmas.
- Not receiving your textbooks until two months after the start of school.
- Falling off a chair or desk while lecturing to a class.
- Running out of paper before an examination.

You might warm up your students with one of your own blessings in disguise, or you might use one of a friend or acquaintance.

Presenting the Unit

The first-level activity is merely a paragraph introducing the concept of a blessing in disguise with a few examples of the phenomenon. If you go over the first section of these units with your classes (we recommend that practice if it seems feasible), ask your students for their own experiences that appeared to be disastrous yet turned out happily. With a little reflection, everyone can come up with a few.

At the second level, the student is to explore the possibility of a happy ending to apparently unfortunate events and circumstances such as becoming ill or having a television set break down. The latter misfortune, we understand, has turned out to be a genuine blessing for some people who never got around to having their set fixed. There are quite a few of these misfortunes to puzzle over, but there is a story in each of them, thus setting up the writing activity at the third level.

The Writing Assignment

Because the student must construct a little plot to figure out how a lost job or a car accident can turn into some sort of blessing, the short story to be written shouldn't lack for inspiration. All the student needs to do is pick the one blessing in disguise that most intrigues him or her and expand the plot that has been hinted at in the response at the second level.

References

Torrance, E. Paul. *The Search for Satori and Creativity.* Buffalo, N.Y.: Bearly Limited, 1979.

Torrance, E. Paul, and H. Tammy Safter. *The Incubation Model of Teaching.* Buffalo, N.Y.: Bearly Limited, 1990.

2 Blessings in Disguise

1. A blessing in disguise is an event or situation that seems to be very unfortunate for an individual, but subsequent events turn it into a blessing. For example, when she was a teenager a famous movie star was a promising dancer, but an injury to her leg ended that career, forcing her to try singing instead. Her singing with a big-name band launched a glittering career in films. One blessing in disguise that we often hear about is the kind where someone misses a scheduled airplane flight and then the airplane crashes. What appears at the time to be an unlucky break turns out to be terribly fortunate.

2. Here are some unfortunate happenings that could possibly become blessings in disguise because of later events. Explain how each could be a blessing in disguise.

An illness

Losing a job

Getting a flat tire

A television set's breaking down

A lapse of memory

Blessings in Disguise *(continued)*

A car accident

A crop failure

Failing an exam

Getting turned down for a date

Not making the football team

Losing an election

Getting lost

A forest fire

3. Future events very often change our perspective of the kindness or cruelty of fate. Actually, even though some people seem always to have things turn out well for them, all of us experience the bitter with the better. After thinking about the above blessings in disguise, you undoubtedly have some good ideas about what events might have taken place in order that one of the misfortunes could become a blessing.

Blessings in Disguise *(continued)*

List the unfortunate events that could become blessings and then convert them into an outline for a short story. Pick the blessing in disguise that most interests you and for which you have the best ideas.

3
Writing a Fortune

An Invitation to Write "Fortunes" for Fortune Cookies

Overview

"Writing a Fortune" begins with an introductory discussion of fortune cookies, which leads into an activity in which your students are to compose their own fortune cookie apothegms.

Creative Thinking Skill to Be Developed: Being Original

Although at first it may seem easy to your students to come up with those short pieces of advice, they may find themselves challenged by the assignment. They will be imitating a distinctive and well-known style, but they also will have to produce ten sayings that are original—and that may prove to be difficult. It probably would be best to put off any sharing of fortune cookie messages until all of your students have written their ten little sayings.

Preparing for the Unit

We presume that all of your students are familiar with fortune cookies, but it is possible that some students haven't had the experience of breaking open a cookie and finding a brief message. Whether or not each student has had a fortune cookie in hand, it would be a very good idea for you to introduce this unit by breaking one open or passing some out in class. Revealing the message will provide a certain amount of suspense and capture the interest of your students.

Presenting the Unit

Probably more than any other unit in this idea book, this unit has a lot of discussion before the student is asked to do any writing. There are only two levels of involvement: the discussion, with a few examples of fortunes, and the writing activity. The writing exercise emerges naturally from the somewhat lengthy discussion of fortune cookies, and then the student is on his or her own.

The Writing Assignment

This unit will appeal especially to those of your students who are partial to short writing assignments. (That might be the majority!) Ten brief "fortunes" are all that the student is invited to write. As with a few of the other units in *What Next?* "Writing a Fortune" is designed to entice the reluctant writer to do a little writing. In this case, it isn't very much. The writing that the student does, however, is not necessarily without challenge or difficulty. It turns out that writing really catchy fortunes is not as easy as it seems.

One of the attractive features of this assignment is that your students can do a variety of things with their fortunes: exchange them, make them into a bulletin board display, put them in a student publication, include them in fortune cookies they actually bake, and so on.

References

Two books by Rexine M. Hayes (available at $2.50 each from the author at 18130 S. Upper Highland Rd., Beavercreek, Oregon 97004) speak plainly to the student about the problems of meeting writing assignments.

Hayes, Rexine M. *The Student Writer.* Beavercreek, Oreg.: 1979.

———. *The Great Theme Scheme and Other Handy Revelations.* Beavercreek, Oreg.: 1981.

3 Writing a Fortune

1. There have been a number of complaints recently that the quality of the messages on the slips of paper in fortune cookies is declining. Slogans, mild insults, and obscure advice often supplant the time-honored and generally felicitous predictions found in the cookies in the past. A recent fortune, "Scar on the conscience is the same as a wound," sounds vaguely Confucian, for instance, but it is nothing to look forward to reading after breaking open a cookie.

The old fortunes were often a bigger treat than the cookies, which were frequently tasteless. Some years ago a person might have kept "Unexpected money and happiness for you soon" indefinitely, not knowing when the good luck would happen. It's unlikely that anyone today would keep "You have forgotten to live by the Golden Rule," a recent message found in a cookie, as a reminder to speak well of others.

The writers of the brief sayings found in fortune cookies are constrained, as are the astrologists who predict tomorrow's events for all of humanity, to phrase their predictions and advice in terms so general that anyone might feel that, just perhaps, the saying does apply to him or her.

2. Perhaps the writing of clever sayings is a lost art, but we doubt that it is. Most of the regular writers of the messages have simply been the everyday employees of the firms that have manufactured the cookies. Imagine that you are given the job of writing a batch of new fortunes for a firm that makes these cookies. Considering what life will be like in the next few years for you and your friends, what ten messages can you invent? You might offer some advice or predict some happy or unhappy event. To produce the ancient and wise Oriental feeling, use fewer than a dozen words for each message. (Please don't use "Help! I'm a prisoner in a Chinese fortune cookie factory!")

Writing a Fortune *(continued*

Here are a few attempts at writing fortunes that may guide you in coming up with ten of your own. You probably can do much better.

Those that know your secret, salute your nobility.
You will always be skillful in games of love and chance.
Despite doubts, events will vindicate your position.
Following unlikely paths leads to discovery.
Through no fault of yours the prize eludes you.

First Attempts

Fortunes Ready for Printing

4
Endangered Human Species

An Invitation to Write an Essay

Overview

The simple idea of the unit (not original, by any means, with us) is that there are certain types of people who are disappearing from the scene in America. A few of these "human endangered species" are offered, somewhat whimsically, in the first section of the unit. The student is to write an essay about his or her favorite (or another type that is more appealing).

Creative Thinking Skill to Be Developed: Looking from a Different Perspective

"Looking from a different perspective" is one of Torrance's eighteen creative thinking skills (Torrance 1979; Torrance and Safter 1990). It is one not found elsewhere in the literature, but some elements of this skill have been written about extensively, especially in the creative problem-solving literature. One aspect is known as "making the familiar strange and the strange familiar." Torrance's skill, however, is more inclusive and encompasses a wider range of techniques for seeing the world differently.

"Analogizing"—making analogies of two things ordinarily not associated with each other—is another aspect of this skill, and essentially that is the approach taken in this unit, that is, naming certain types of humans as endangered species in the way animals are so designated.

Preparing for the Unit

Any comment about an endangered species could be a good lead-in for administering this unit. Since there is so much discussion of the plight of animals and plants as a result of pollution, reduction of rain forests, overfishing, and so on, you might not have to bring up the topic. However, if you see a propitious time for using the unit and no comment about endangered species is forthcoming, you can make an appropriate statement or ask a pertinent question about one of the many topics of concern in the general field of ecology. Unfortunately, these problems aren't going to go away, and we can't kid ourselves about two things: they are serious and we need more knowledge to solve them.

Presenting the Unit

"Endangered Human Species" is an easy unit to administer. It consists of only two parts: an introduction of the concept with an offering of seven human types that are dying out, and an invitation to write an essay about one of the types (or another type of the student's choosing).

If the seven species don't seem provocative or appropriate enough, please substitute some of your own. There are lots of candidates in our society, and we always encourage you to change the unit in any way that you think will improve it for your students.

References

Torrance, E. Paul. *The Search for Satori and Creativity.* Buffalo, N.Y.: Bearly Limited, 1979.

Torrance, E. Paul, and H. Tammy Safter. *The Incubation Model of Teaching.* Buffalo, N.Y.: Bearly Limited, 1990.

4 Endangered Human Species

1. We read and hear a lot about endangered species of animals and plants, but as we enter the twenty-first century it would seem that there are other things that are in danger of becoming very scarce. What about people who write personal letters—not people who promptly reply to letters but just people who write personal letters? We know a great many people who haven't written a personal letter in years. And there are any number of other people who are members of, as they used to say, "a dying breed."

Do you write personal letters? _____yes _____no

If so, how often?____

Which of these types of people do you consider to be extremely rare—and getting rarer?

- The person who, when realizing he or she has dialed the wrong number, stays on the phone and apologizes (instead of hanging up when an unfamiliar voice says "hello").
- The child who would rather read than play video games.
- The Scout who helps a little old person across the street (when the old person is willing to be escorted).
- Car dealers who don't want to be the stars of their television commercials.
- The white-collar worker who wears a hat to work.
- People who refuse to wear very revealing clothing.

Endangered Human Species *(continued)*

2. Select one of the above endangered species—or another of which you are acutely aware.

Write an essay about the problem (if, indeed, it is a problem). Review your first draft and then revise it so that it might be suitable for an editorial in a newspaper or magazine. You can write your outline in the space that follows.

5
War

An Invitation to Write a Ten-Minute Talk

Overview

The first two sections of the unit discuss war as a concept, ending by questioning your students about how the urge to dominate might manifest itself in the twenty-first century. In the final section, we invite your students to prepare a ten-minute talk to a service club about one of the topics dealt with in the previous section.

Creative Thinking Skills to Be Developed: Elaborating; Being Original

For most students, planning a speech is an arduous chore, and delivering one is a harrowing experience. We're not asking your students for more than a script for a speech. Nevertheless, this writing assignment will be undertaken willingly by a majority of your students only if the topic of war (aggression, domination, belligerence, and so on) "grabs" them. We believe that the experience of getting an idea and developing it will be helpful to them in future curricular and noncurricular endeavors.

In *The Incubation Model of Teaching*, Torrance (Torrance and Safter 1990) states that "the ability to add details to a product or an idea is an important one. The ability to elaborate and work out plans, implement and sell solutions is particularly important. It is not enough to have a great idea. It must be elaborated to become of value" (p. 55). By getting an idea about the forces that result in war in the second section and then expanding it into a speech, your students will have engaged in a practical exercise in elaborating.

Preparing for the Unit

The tragic fact that wars are always with us is really not the focus of this exercise. It is that conflict comes in many forms. Students are encouraged to try to understand some of the reasons for conflict and then to look into one of the common antithetical situations in society. Having done some thinking about one of the "wars" that are going on continually within society, students are invited to write a ten-minute talk about the conflict.

There may be a "gas war" or a "gang war" in the news that you can use to introduce this unit, but if not, you can doubtless lead in to the unit by a reference to or a discussion of one of the multifarious conflicts, some quite violent and others only cerebral, that occur in society. Our form of government is based on balancing opposing forces, and very often it appears as if the clashing of sides or interests is necessary to keep the engine of democracy fired up. Interestingly enough, a "conflict of interest" for someone in government is one of the worst things to have—individuals, within themselves, are not supposed to represent more than one position or allegiance. There should be any number of curricular and extracurricular happenings, then, that tie in with this unit.

Presenting the Unit

At the warm-up stage or first level of involvement in this unit, the student is presented with the use of the term *war* in athletic circles. In recent years, the metaphor has been taken all too seriously by spectators who have fought with each other in the stands and now and then with the contestants on the playing field. This behavior may or may not have plagued the amateur and professional games that have been played recently in your area, but the reasons for such behavior have disturbed all but the hooligans who engage in the brawls. After the brief introduction of the topic, the student is asked to come up with his or her own definition of the word *war.*

At the second level of involvement, the student is to compare the internal wars of the community—"price wars" and "gang wars"—with wars between nations. Then you introduce the idea that there are legal and illegal ways to wage war. After discussing the legality of war, the student is asked how the urge to dominate will manifest itself in seven arenas—wars between the sexes, industrial giants, nations, religious groups, political parties, ethnic groups, and the landed and landless—in the next century. Unless we are mistaken, this section of the unit is worthy of considerable time on the part of individual students as well as of the group.

There are several advantages to discussing the issues raised in this unit with your class as a whole before individual students begin their separate investigations of the weighty topics that are presented. As the authors imagine a typical classroom situation, assignments are generally preceded by discussions, and then there are discussions with individual members of the class and with the entire group, depending upon the nature of the assignment. This is the kind of activity that seems to require both kinds of discussion.

The Writing Assignment

This exercise provides the opportunity for you to point out the essential elements of a good speech. Since the talk to be written out is not terribly long, it should be carefully planned and hard-hitting. There is time only for an opening, a thesis, and a closing. The number of points to be made will be relatively few, and so they must be the most important that the student can find. Accordingly, if the speech isn't to be a collection of personal opinions, the student must do some research. The observations of the speaker-writer are important, of course, but he or she should also interview others, read periodicals and books, listen to recordings, and view films and filmstrips.

After gathering facts, the student must organize his or her thoughts into a sequential pattern, and this calls for a rough outline. In all probability, this outline should be revised. You may want to review the first drafts of your students' outlines.

Depending upon the skills and maturity of your students, the final products might actually be presented as ten-minute talks to the class. They can be made informally from notes or the outline, or they can simply be read aloud.

References

Dennis K. Renner, associate professor of English at Gannon University, has written an excellent article about the writing skills involved in the research assignment. Renner provides an index of the sequential tasks necessary to do satisfactory research writing.

Renner, Dennis K. "Teaching the Research Assignment in the 1980s." *The Clearing House* 59 (September 1980): 19–23.

Fred M. Amram and Frank T. Benson, University of Minnesota, have published a student's workbook to help speech writers apply knowledge about the creative problem-solving process to the creation of speeches.

Amram, F. M., and F. T. Benson. *Creating a Speech.* New York: Charles Scribner's, 1968.

Torrance, E. Paul, and H. Tammy Safter. *The Incubation Model of Teaching.* Buffalo, N.Y.: Bearly Limited, 1990.

5 War

1. Before a recent football game, a coach stated emotionally, "It'll be a war!" Baseball coaches and players—and boxers, of course—have been known to talk that way, too.

Exactly what do coaches and others mean when they say that the contest coming up will be a war?

Without looking in a dictionary, give your definition of war.

2. You have heard about the wars against poverty, ignorance, and disease. We have "price wars" between retail stores and gasoline stations and "gang wars" between groups of youth in cities.

How are the conflicts described here different from the wars between countries that are continually happening around the world?

War *(continued)*

How are such conflicts like the armed conflicts between nations and between religious groups?

Perhaps the purpose of war is to establish domination over others. There are legal ways to wage war, and there are illegal ways.

What are several of the legal forms of warfare?

What are several of the illegal forms of warfare?

How might the urge to dominate express itself between nations in the next century?

Between the sexes?

Between competing industrial giants?

Between political parties?

Between religious groups?

Between ethnic groups?

Between those with land and those without land?

3. Imagine that it is twenty years from now and you are to give a ten-minute talk to a local service club. Your topic is one of the types of conflicts that you have discussed above. What would you say? Because you don't want to be misquoted in the media, you write out your remarks ahead of time.

Outline your talk about conflict, noting the points you particularly want to stress, and then write out your speech. You'll want to do some research about this "war" so that you can support your points with facts. You may use the space below for the outline of your speech.

6
Lunar Follies

An Invitation to Write a Review for a Newspaper

Overview

This is the type of activity that is given to young people who participate in the Future Problem Solving competitions. The students are given a number of facts—in this case, about colonizing the moon—and then they are asked to identify problems and offer solutions to them. For "Lunar Follies," your students are asked to write a review of a musical extravaganza for a newspaper published on the moon.

Creative Thinking Skills to Be Developed: Seeing Relationships; Being Original

No one can really know what will happen with regard to our making use of the moon, but we can make educated guesses, based on our knowledge and analyses of pertinent data and projections of trends. The basic skill involved in the activity and in writing a hypothetical review of a musical is seeing relationships.

Preparing for and Presenting the Unit

"Lunar Follies" can be used effectively in conjunction with curricular activities featuring the study of the solar system, space exploration, gravity, population problems, energy, and musical entertainment. The topic of space travel inevitably brings up a number of problems about our ability to survive on other planets and space bodies. Problems of coping in an alien environment include psychological as well as physical factors.

You might want to go over the first part of the unit with your students, engaging them in a discussion of how colonists on the moon would utilize their leisure time. For the writing exercise, students can then use their own ideas about what the major features of a review of a lunar musical extravaganza might be.

The Writing Assignment

It would probably be a good idea to have a discussion before the writing assignment in which you determine how well acquainted your students are with reviews of entertainment in the media. If they are not well acquainted with reviews, a logical way of handling the writing assignment is to have your students read several reviews in newspapers and magazines before they do any writing. Most major newspapers carry reviews of concerts, movies, books, television programs, nightclub acts, and so on. You can point out the role of the critic in reviewing performances. Reviews of theatrical events purportedly often determine the success, or lack thereof, of plays and musicals.

6 Lunar Follies

1. Some experts of space travel have expressed the belief that underground lunar colonies will be established within the next thirty years. These colonies will deal with metal mining and lunar research. Also, radio telescopes and x-ray telescopes will be among the first permanent installations on the lunar surface. A great deal of synthetic food will be used, though some things could be raised under artificial light. Solar generators will provide the electrical energy needed. Lunar gravity can be employed in easing the difficulty of lifting heavy loads. Surface transportation will be common, but the shuttling of large numbers of people or quantities of products will not be feasible for at least another century. Therefore, colonists will be establishing a new life for themselves, not merely staying for a short period of time.

The colonists will have to find ways of amusing themselves when they are not engaged in their jobs, and so they will bring games and musical instruments from Earth. Those among the colonists who have talents in the fields of acting, music, dance, and humor will entertain the others. Entertainment events will be regularly scheduled throughout the year. Everyone will avidly read newspapers carrying news of happenings on the moon and on Earth.

Lunar Follies *(continued)*

2. Suppose that you are employed by the largest of the newspapers on the moon. Your assignment one lunar evening is to review a musical extravaganza that is being performed in a large underground theater. There are a number of features of the musical that differ from those performed on Earth. The performers make many references to the special ways people live on the moon. Write up your review of the evening's proceedings with several of these differences in mind. You might also take into consideration the special physical limitations that living on the moon imposes.

Outline your review of the lunar extravaganza in the space below.

7
For Sale

An Invitation to Write a Short Story

Overview

Your students are presented with a little story about a house that has a "FOR SALE" sign in the front yard, and then they are asked to speculate about the reasons the house is for sale. After listing various events that could have led to the house's being put up for sale, they are invited to expand their ideas into a short story.

Creative Thinking Skills to Be Developed: Elaborating; Being Original

As is the case with "War," your students are led from ruminating about a topic to expanding upon it. Instead of creating a ten-minute talk, in this unit they are invited to elaborate their ideas into a short story.

"For Sale" relies upon the curiosity we all have when we witness something changing for the worse. When things deteriorate, disintegrate, or fall into disrepute or disrepair, we are saddened a little, even if those changes don't affect us directly. Most of us make up hypotheses in order to account in our own minds for such changes, and it is that element of human nature to which we hope to appeal in this unit.

Preparing for the Unit

The little story that introduces the writing exercise should sound familiar to your students, whether they live in a rural or an urban area. It could probably be told by people in every part of the country. More and more people are offering their personal possessions for sale. Some individuals are making a business of having garage sales, acting as brokers for neighbors and friends in selling castoffs. In many instances people just wish to get rid of articles that aren't being used and are taking up space. But in other cases there is a story behind the act of offering an article for sale.

Any of these observations could be brought to your students' attention before you administer this unit. The activity might follow a bake sale at school or an occasion when someone in the class, or connected with it in some way, offers anything for sale. You might contrive to offer something for sale yourself, but not for money.

Early in the year, you can introduce your students to short, simple writing exercises in order to help them learn to rely upon their own insights for inspiration. Here are seven "quickie" themes that you can present a week or so before a unit such as "For Sale" is given.

- Describe two sounds you heard just after you awoke this morning. Were they related in any way?
- What is the color you like least? Why don't you like it?
- Who has the best-sounding name that you know? Why does it sound good?
- If you close your eyes and think of your best friend, what image do you have?
- What is the very first sign of autumn's coming for you?
- When do you sense the first sign of autumn?
- Describe the way one of your classmates leaves this classroom.
- Who has the warmest smile on television? Why do you think so?

Presenting the Unit

"For Sale" consists of a short narrative about the occupants of a house who periodically offer their possessions for sale, an activity in which the students speculate as to the events that might have brought about the sales, and an invitation to write a story about the people in "the white house by the side of the highway." This unit is rather straightforward, then, in leading students to a writing exercise that derives directly from the narrative that they have just read.

Perhaps the only serious problem you might have in coaxing your students to write entertaining short stories is that there may be a sameness about their solutions to the puzzle. It would be most effective if you could ask a few questions that might open up the possibilities inherent in the narrative. For example, you can ask

- Do you suppose that the people who live in the house are all related?
- Do you think that they benefited from a series of lucky breaks? (The tendency will be for your students to imagine that a series of *misfortunes* befell the occupants.)
- Is there any pattern to the kinds of things they offered for sale? Why do you think so?
- Did you expect that the house would be the final possession offered for sale?
- If the house were not the last thing to be sold, what would be?
- Would you have a better story if the item you listed were the last thing with a "FOR SALE" sign on it? Why or why not?

The Writing Assignment

Although it allows the students to devise a plot for the story as they see fit, this writing exercise is rather structured in the sense that students are to imagine the events that had led to the sale of the many possessions the people chose to sell, and then to construct a plot with these events as its framework.

It is quite possible that the story won't particularly inspire your students to do some plot building. On the other hand, as an exercise in writing a short story, "For Sale" has the virtue of allowing your students to go from their speculations into the writing exercise without the hand-wringing and fretting in which many students engage when they are asked to write a short story. In other words, if they can hypothesize about the events that led to the sale of the items or about the personalities of the people in the white house (which is perhaps more important), your students will be well on their way to having a plot in hand.

The alternative to presenting the exercise as we devised it is to permit your students to write about another puzzling event. There could be any number of incidents that have perplexed them. Puzzling events happen all of the time, of course. Here are a few that they might have experienced:

- The nonappearance of a street vendor who had been selling his or her wares at the same place for years.
- A band-aid on the cheek of a lovely young girl.
- The sudden appearance of deer in a very desolate area.
- Seeing a person who looks very familiar but whose hair and nose don't appear to be the way you remembered them.
- A sudden, unexplained silence on the radio.
- Finding a store closed that had always been open on weekday afternoons.

7 For Sale

1. "In our neck of the woods," the portly little man said, "people are always selling things. You see all kinds of things with a 'For Sale' sign hung on them, from cars and wood to baby carriages and vegetables. Sometimes, though, I get to wondering what reasons people have for getting rid of the things they do. I was just thinking of the first time I passed that white house alongside the highway and saw a 'For Sale' on a utility trailer. A few months later I saw a similar sign—maybe the same one—on the windshield of a pickup truck. A little later, there was a sign in the front yard announcing that there was a horse that could be purchased if someone was interested. Not too much after, a sign appeared advertising a motorcycle for sale, and the lawn sure needed mowing. Then, there was a tent with probably that same sign on it.

"I didn't pass by the house for a year since I got another job and didn't come that way anymore. When I did drive by one Sunday two years later, I noticed that the house now looked real rundown. It needed a lot of attention, and there was a new 'For Sale' sign—one put there by the Mertens Realty people. Yeah, the house was for sale. I've always wondered about that family."

2. Do you know any stories similar to this tale? It probably isn't too much different from many others. Can you imagine why the occupants of the white house were always selling things? Perhaps you can think of some events that might have happened to those people.

In the space below, list the events you think might have caused the people to sell their things.

For Sale *(continued)*

3. Why don't you put those events into a story about the people in the white house? Having done some thinking about them, you should be able to write a short story that will interest both you and those who read it.

Outline your plot of the story in the space below. Then write your story on separate sheets of paper.

8
Spoiled

An Invitation to Describe an Invention

Overview

From time to time the word *spoiled* has been commonly used to refer to children. It isn't currently especially in favor, but as a concept it is a most interesting one. It also is used frequently in reference to contaminated food, but it is also used when saying that anything is tainted, blighted, or ruined.

After being asked to think of the implications of different things being spoiled, the student is asked to give a definition of the word. Then he or she is asked to consider whether something once spoiled can be restored to its original condition.

Let's consider the items we gave the student to mull over:

- **a dance**—Mistakes on the part of either partner when performing a dance is an obvious answer, but the student may construe "dance" as a social event rather than an individual or a couple dancing to music.
- **a poem**—Poems can be spoiled by any number of mistakes, from poor endings to bad rhythms.
- **a conversation**—An unthinking remark, domination by one party, a slur, and so on might come to your students' minds.
- **a painting**—"Poor" use of colors, faulty technique, imbalance, and so on could come to the minds of your students.
- **a dish of food**—Too much salt spoils a dish for some people; too much sugar or cooking spoils a dish for others.
- **a game**—Your students might think of poor sportsmanship and biased refereeing.

- **a party**—A good way to spoil a party is to have an argument or fight, but your students will come up with other reasons.
- **a friendship**—Borrowing is an excellent way to ruin a friendship, but your students may think of thoughtlessness, jealousy, misunderstandings, and so on.
- **a town**—A great many towns are spoiled because of a lack of planning; some people say towns and cities are ruined because of demographic changes; important companies desert towns and cause economic hardships.
- **a country**—It takes a good deal more than population shifts, the relocation of industries, and haphazard planning to spoil a country, but the perception that a country is a good deal worse than it used to be may not be an exaggeration; droughts, famines, and wars do much to make life less worthwhile in many countries.

The second part of the unit invites the student to come up with ways that a variety of things can be spoiled. After considering how diverse phenomena can be changed for the worse, the student is asked to think in much larger dimensions. How are we making life less satisfactory—or perhaps miserable—for future generations? The student is to come up with a plausible invention that will make life less hazardous and more enjoyable for children who have yet to be born.

Preparing for the Unit

With regard to the unit's serious message, the deteriorating condition of the planet, there should be many opportunities for leading into the unit (or having the unit complement and reinforce a curriculum topic). If we are to believe the environmentalists and "preservationists" who are quoted so often in our newspapers and magazines (less often on television and radio), humankind is in trouble. There should be no dearth of media items that would lead into "Spoiled" very nicely. On the other hand, occasions when students are spoiling situations for others can be used to emphasize the many sociological elements in the unit.

Presenting the Unit

If there is a discussion after the unit is given to your students, you will play a key role. In all likelihood, there will be many reactions to the first two sections of the unit. The reactions may become emotional, or they may be on a dispassionate, intellectual level.

The first section may not provoke strong feelings because your students are likely to perceive others as being spoiled rather than themselves. In the second section, your students may have had recent experiences that will elicit heated comments. If you have your students respond to the third section individually, you might encourage them to come up with plausible, rather than fantastic or silly, ideas for inventions that will improve humankind's lot in the decades to come. There are those students who welcome an opportunity to become unruly or to "show off" when you give them any invitation to give free rein to their imaginations. Your encouragement can lead even these students to think about inventions that might really ameliorate the growing problems of ozone depletion, pollution, and the skyrocketing national debt.

8 Spoiled

1. Have you ever been "spoiled?" What does it mean to be spoiled?

Write your definition of "spoiled" in the space below.

Do you know anyone who is terribly spoiled? _____yes _____no
If so, why is that person spoiled?

What else can be spoiled besides people?

Is spoiling irreversible? Once spoiled, are things always spoiled? For instance, is the spoiled child doomed to be flawed all of his or her life?

Spoiled *(continued)*

2. Name at least one way of spoiling the following:

a dance

a poem

a conversation

a painting

a dish of food

a game

a party

a friendship

a town

a country

3. We hear a good deal about making it tough for generations yet unborn by adding to the national debt, polluting rivers and oceans, and depleting the ozone layer. In other words, the people who populate this nation and others are spoiling things for future generations.

What invention might help greatly in making life better rather than worse for future generations? Describe the invention and tell how it would improve the lives of young people who haven't been born yet.

9
Try to Remember

An Invitation to Write a Poem

Overview

"Try to Remember" is about memories of feelings. At the beginning, your students are asked to recall experiences that cause them to have seven different emotions. Then they are asked to predict which of those experiences they will most likely remember in ten years. Next, they are to predict what experiences ten years hence will make them feel very happy, quite proud, resentful, awfully puzzled, and very contented. Finally, they are invited to write a poem based on one or more of the feelings about which they have been thinking.

Creative Thinking Skill to Be Developed: Being Original

The kind of creativity called for in this unit is of a high order; that is, writing poetry—genuine poetry—demands sensitivity, imagination, and discipline. If the writer is lucky, there will be a good dose of inspiration mixed in, too. We don't make such a big deal out of writing poems in this book, however. Most teachers are very happy to get just a glimmer of a metaphor or a rudimentary allusion from a majority of their students. What they can be sure of getting is a lot of rhyme.

Preparing and Presenting the Unit

"Try to Remember" begins with an activity in which the student is to recollect various emotions experienced in the past year, and so a good lead-in would be a brief discussion of the varying abilities of people to remember, or a discussion about feelings. Since adolescence is a time when emotions are given a lot of attention, there should be quite a bit of interest in recalling events that made your students feel angry, frustrated, grief-stricken, and so on. Not that all of your students will particularly want to share their experiences. Some will, but the others should be allowed not to divulge their keen disappointment, embarrassments, and fears if they are unwilling to do so.

At the second level, your students are asked to imagine what events will cause them to experience other emotions ten years hence. This is a trickier task because they will have to project who they will be and what they will be doing in their late twenties. They may or may not have given much thought to being that age. As we know, a person of thirty is middle-aged to a sixteen-year-old.

The Writing Assignment

The final level of involvement of "Try to Remember" is the writing of a poem. If you have allowed your students a large measure of privacy during the first two parts of the exercise, you might also permit them to keep their responses to themselves when they have finished their poems, if they so wish.

We are leaving entirely up to you the crucial matter of what form of poetry your students are to choose in writing their poems. For some young people, a poem isn't a poem unless it has rhyme. There is nothing wrong with rhymes unless the sole purpose of putting the lines together turns out to be to have them rhyme. Too many students write that kind of "poem." When this assignment is coordinated with a unit about poetry, the type of poetry being studied can be the form that serves as a model for your students.

Writing poetry doesn't appeal to every student, obviously enough, but you should encourage all of your students to give it a try. Some will surprise themselves, most pleasantly. We have included other forms of poetry in this idea book (the quintet and haiku), and so your students can refer to those forms if they wish. Although haiku is meant to have nature as its theme, it might appeal to some students because of its brevity. If they use that form, you could just make a silent apology to the Japanese for the transgression. Cinquains, on the other hand, are also brief, and there is no accepted restriction on subject matter. Both the haiku and the cinquain are popular because, in addition to being short, they don't require a rhyme pattern and it is relatively easy to conceive ideas for them.

Following is an example of a cinquain with the applicable characteristics listed by each line.

Wonder: One word (two syllables) that is usually the title or subject.

Perception's torch: Two words (four syllables) describing the subject.

Enlightening, exciting minds: Three words (six syllables) expressing a feeling.

Striving desperately to know: Four words (eight syllables) expressing an action.

Questions: Another word (two syllables) for the subject, or the subject revealed.

The so-called classical cinquain imitates the haiku in requiring the pattern of a set number of syllables for each line, but teachers have found that having students attempt to use the 1-2-3-4-1 word pattern is generally more successful. In fact, it is wise not to stress the pattern as much as the rhythm and imagery in both haiku and cinquains.

9 Try to Remember

1. Our memories are selective, and, fortunately, we tend to remember the good happenings more than the bad ones. Thinking back to your experiences of ten years ago, you'll probably recall more pleasant happenings than unpleasant ones. Let's not go back that far, though. Why don't you think about your experiences of the past year? During the last twelve months, what experiences caused you to feel

Elation?

Embarrassment?

Grief?

Chagrin?

Frustration?

Anger?

Accomplishment?

Can you predict which of these experiences you will most readily recall ten years from now? Which one would it be?

Try to Remember *(continued)*

2. Now that you have done some thinking about the past, why don't you think about the future? You can't predict the future with certainty, of course, but why don't you try? Ten years from now, what kind of experience will make you feel

Very happy?

Quite proud?

Resentful?

Awfully puzzled?

Very contented?

If you still have these predictions and remember to look back at them ten years from now, you could receive quite a jolt. What seems terribly important now may not seem nearly so significant in ten years.

Try to Remember *(continued)*

3. Since you have been thinking and writing about your emotions—both past and future—why don't you select one of these feelings and encapsulate it in a poem? The poem can rhyme, or it might be free verse. To be successful as a poem, it should communicate the essence of your feelings in relatively few words. Some poems are lengthy ballads that are fundamentally narratives, but you should not really try to tell the whole story in your poem as Tennyson or Longfellow did. A good rule is to simplify your phrases, rather than attempt to make them fancy.

You can start work on your poem about a feeling in the space below. Unless you are very fortunate, you will have to revise your stanzas several times, but be persistent and try to finish with a poem you can feel some pride in.

10
Acronyms Corrupt Honorable English (ACHE)

An Invitation to Invent Futuristic Acronyms

Overview

This unit is designed to be a light-hearted exercise in inventing acronyms. It starts with a discussion of the use and overuse of calling everything by its initials. Your students are then asked to produce bogus words for seven well-known acronyms. Finally, they are to dream up five acronyms of the future.

Creative Thinking Skills to Be Developed: Combining Ideas and Elements; Being Original

At one level, this unit simply invites your students to come up with some amusing acronyms, combining words in ways that make a little sense and some humor. At another level, students will have to do some serious thinking in order to imagine what the IRAs, NOWs, and VIPs of the future will be.

Preparing for the Unit

If you wait until a student uses an acronym in class, you probably won't have to wait too long. On such an occasion you can point out that our conversations and communications are riddled with initials. Sometimes it seems we want to shorten and hasten everything in our lives except its longevity. Of course, many organizations are named the way they are just so they can be reduced to an acronym. Some are especially appropriate, such as the women's unit of the navy in World War II, the WAVE. Others are contrived in an obvious, and often clumsy, way.

Presenting the Unit

After leading into the unit with a few brief comments about acronyms, you can put your students on their own to tackle this unit. If some genuine humor is engendered, you can have a class discussion following the first section of the unit, and your students can reveal their ideas for remaking the names of the organizations and expressions we have offered. You may have some qualms about the nature of some of your students' offerings; therefore, it might be a good idea to ask them to keep their acronyms within the bounds of good taste. If they apply themselves a little, the final section concerning acronyms of the future can lead to further learning experiences.

10 Acronyms Corrupt Honorable English (ACHE)

1. We have a downright mania for reducing the names of organizations, processes, diseases, corporations, schools, and other things to initials. And each year it gets worse. There is ESP and also ESPN. We have NIT and NET, TNT and TBA, AAA and AARP, PTA and ATV, NASCAR and NBA. It's better to have TDs than DTs. It goes on and on. Many years ago the accepted nickname for Reserve Officers Training Corps, ROTC, was "Rotten Old Tin Cans." For all we know, the much maligned ROTC may still be called that.

Giving alternative and crazy names to acronyms is an amusing pastime. (Acronyms are initials that spell a word.) Would you like to try? Can you come up with alternative, humorous names for these acronyms?

WASP
NOW
IRA
MADD
SAP
MASH
GATT

Acronyms Corrupt Honorable English *(continued)*

2. Will this malady of using initials instead of names keep on spreading? What will be the acronyms of the future?

Make up five organizations, substances, processes, and/or sayings that might be prominent in fifty years. The first letter of the words should combine to make up one word for each name.

1. ______________________________

   ____

2. ______________________________

   ____

3. ______________________________

   ____

4. ______________________________

   ____

5. ______________________________

   ____

11
Like That

An Invitation to Invent Similes

Overview

There is a discussion of similes at the outset of the unit, and a number of examples of that figure of speech are given. Then various occupational workers are compared in pairs ("How can a baseball player be like a firefighter?"). The unit ends with an invitation to your students to produce five similes of the future.

Creative Thinking Skill to Be Developed: Seeing Relationships

Although using similes is quite natural to almost any speaker of English, the similes called for in this unit require some mind stretching. The relationships to be made explicit in the first part of the unit are rarely, if ever, expressed ("How can a ballroom dancer be like a stamp collector?"), and those at the end of the unit have yet to be expressed.

Preparing for the Unit

This unit about similes deals with the figure of speech that every student is most familiar with, but it has two unusual features. It asks the student to look for common qualities in people as diverse as ballroom dancers and stamp collectors, and the unit also invites the student to produce similes that might possibly be used in the next century. Therefore, it would be a good idea to present this unit at a time when your class is interested in figures of speech and idiomatic expressions and is also in a mood to play around with language.

Presenting the Unit

At the first level, the student reads about the nature of a simile and is presented with a number of examples of very common "as" and "like" similes. This warming-up section is designed to set the stage for the second-level activity of discovering traits that various types of people have in common. The student will probably be aware, in responding to the six comparisons, that they form a chain; that is, the comparisons start and end with the baseball player. Incidentally, the first comparison of the baseball player and the firefighter was used deliberately because a relief pitcher in baseball has long been known as a fireman. From there on, however, the comparisons are fairly obscure. If your students are to complete this part of the unit, they will have to do some thinking.

If you believe that the comparisons are too difficult for members of your class, you can substitute these more obvious ones or others that you make up.

- How is an elevator operator like a pilot?
- How is a sales person like a preacher?
- How is an architect like a sculptor?
- How is a cook like a poet?
- How is a lion tamer like a teacher?
- How is an accountant like a tightrope walker?

The Writing Assignment

The third level is comprised of an invitation to invent similes for a future time. Throughout the units of this idea book, we attempt to have your students think about what their world will be like in twenty, thirty, or forty years. Asking them to imagine expressions that will be common in the next century will cause them to consider what will be very familiar then that is almost unknown now. If we are successful in motivating your students to speculate on this matter, they should be susceptible to the suggestion that they do a good deal of reading.

The following are some of the more commonly available magazines devoted entirely or largely to future concepts, problems, and predictions:

The Futurist	*Science*
Omni	*Science Digest*
Next	*Quest*
Discover	*L-5 News*

Reference

Synectics, Inc. *Making It Strange: A New Design for Creative Thinking and Writing: Teacher's Manual.* New York: Harper & Row, 1968.

11 Like That

1. In a recent telecast of a football game the announcer commented after one play, "The tackler was draped over the ball carrier like a cheap suit." It was good, graphic language, if not good grammar. In describing what we see, hear, feel, smell, and taste, we often compare animate objects with inanimate objects. This figure of speech, the simile, is probably the most frequently used of all the devices of language. Using *as* and *like,* we compare one thing with another. An instant image is brought to mind when a simile is used because of the universally recognized characteristic of the thing being used for purposes of comparison. We all know immediately what quality someone or something has when he, she, or it is like "a bolt out of the blue," a "cat on a hot tin roof," "a chicken with its head cut off," or "a child in a candy shop." With other similes the quality is made explicit: "meek as a lamb," "slippery as an eel," "sharp as a tack," "stubborn as a mule," "hungry as a horse," "clumsy as an ox," "hard as a rock," and so on.

2. We can compare all kinds of things that don't have such obvious characteristics in common; if we do, we can get insights that aren't gained by using the usual similes. For example, if you compare working in a factory with being in a house of horrors, the idea of being beset by a series of bad experiences is communicated quickly. Now, let's see what various kinds of people have in common.

How can a baseball player be like a fireman?

How can a fireman be like a hitchhiker?

How can a hitchhiker be like a ballroom dancer?

How can a ballroom dancer be like a stamp collector?

How can a stamp collector be like a Republican?

How can a Republican be like a baseball player?

Like That *(continued)*

3. It is possible that new expressions will come into the English language as our lives change during the coming decades. Thinking about the future, see if you can invent similes for these things. Complete these expressions:

__________ like a quark.

As _____________ as a time warp.

________________ like a clone.

________________ like a laser.

As _______________ as a computer.

Can you think of any other expressions that might be quite common in the decades to come?

Write them down here if you can.

12
Sweet Success

An Invitation to Write an Essay

Overview

After being introduced to the topic of our society's preoccupation with the idea of success, your students are asked to find the common measures of success through a dozen activities and characteristics. Next, the students are asked how enduring those measures will be. Then we add a question about when success is not so sweet. Finally, your students are asked what measure of success they feel especially strongly about, and we invite them to write an essay about that measure of success.

Creative Thinking Skills to Be Developed: Seeing Relationships; Being Original

There is as much critical thinking as creative thinking in this unit. Your students are asked to analyze carefully a very important concept in our culture: sweet success. The measures by which we determine success are examined from several angles, and then your students are invited to write an essay about one measure of success. A central idea underlying this unit is that the way we view success greatly influences our behavior.

Preparing the Unit

Since the emphasis upon success is so much a part of our national ethos, it is hardly necessary to spend a great deal of time leading into this unit. On the other hand, it will work best if an occasion has arisen when the subject of success has become a matter of consequence for the young men and women in your classes. Contests of all sorts punctuate the school year, and we imagine there is hardly a week that goes by that groups of students are not successful or unsuccessful in some quest. On the individual level, there is a continual striving for success. One could say there is a mania for success (but with some people, also a fear of it); and the results of the obsession are all around us, in every facet of modern living.

Presenting the Unit

The initial activity of the unit involves the student in naming the measures we have for a dozen endeavors, ranging from being strong to recording a song. Actually, hundreds of endeavors could be listed, and you may well want to ask about several that are important to you or your students. Most of the responses will fall into two categories—awards and formal recognition or informal recognition. We give awards for so many endeavors that your students will probably find that there are awards for just about anything that is legitimate if they investigate the matter.

At the second level, the student is asked about his or her feelings concerning these measures of success. You may want to conduct a rather penetrating discussion of the measures we have for success.

Implicit in any discussion of success is the idea of failure. This opposing experience, which is far more frequent than success in a great many endeavors, is a concept that can be delved into at this point. For instance, if there are fifteen competitors in a race, are there fourteen competitors who have failed when the race is finished? According to many athletes, the American public has generally answered affirmatively, even for the individuals who place second, third, and fourth. This attitude is most evident during Olympics years. Our philosophy about winning and losing is slowly undergoing a slight change. Will this trend continue? Your students may have some opinions about whether winning will be everything (or the "only thing," as several football coaches have affirmed) in the next century.

The Writing Assignment

When the student has reached the final section of the unit, he or she should have begun to have a few notions about our society's attitudes concerning success and failure. The invitation to write an essay about one of the measures of success discussed at the first two levels may not be taken eagerly, but it is likely that the student has some firmly held opinions about at least one of the measures.

The student might prefer to write about other measures of success for different kinds of activities. Other endeavors that are given considerable recognition in our society include

- Winning an election
- Getting your name in the *Guinness Book of Records*
- Losing twenty-five pounds
- Finishing a marathon
- Baking the best cake at the fair
- Being named the most popular girl or boy
- Having a winning ticket for the Irish Sweepstakes
- Celebrating a fiftieth wedding anniversary
- Purchasing a Cadillac
- And many, many others

Reference

Dwyer, Wayne. *The Sky's the Limit.* New York: Simon and Schuster, 1980.

12 Sweet Success

1. The idea of success is always with us. Either consciously or unconsciously, we are concerned with success most of the time. There are many ways of determining success. Can you think of a few?

Name them.

More and more awards are being given these days. In fact, television has accentuated the trend by giving sports awards such as "Player of the Game," "Player of the Series," "Player of the Tournament," "Defensive Player of the Game," "Offensive Player of the Game," and "Player of the Year" awards in profusion.

What measures of success do we have for

Being successful in business?

Writing prose and poetry?

Sweet Success *(continued)*

Promoting peace?

Engineering automobiles?

Getting good grades in school?

Being very attractive?

Playing the piano well?

Being strong?

Recording a song?

Performing an act of heroism?

Televising a situation comedy?

Being a good citizen?

Which of these measures will last longest?

Which measure will not last much longer?

Which measure will last for a very long time but really shouldn't?

Is there some endeavor that we should have an award for but currently don't?

There are times when success is not sweet. Can you think of one or two of these? Name them.

Which measure of success do you feel most strongly about? What kind of attention do you think should be given to this kind of success in future years?

Why do you feel so strongly about this measure of success?

2. Why don't you write an essay about it? Here are the essential elements of an essay:

- The essay is written about one special subject.
- It is written from a particular point of view; the interpretations are the writer's.
- Facts are marshaled to support contentions or arguments.
- The most important points are made at the beginning and at the end.

Sweet Success *(continued)*

Here is some space you can use for jotting down ideas and for outlining your essay.

13
Tracking the Mind

An Invitation to Describe a Mental Activity

Overview

In a sense, the first two parts of this unit deal entirely with metaphor, the metaphor of the human mind behaving as an athlete behaves. Since metaphors don't have to be exact, and since their main value is pointing up some likeness, we can get away with this extended metaphor even though we know that the mind operates in ways far more complicated than leapfrogging, hopping, or running.

The second and third sections put the spotlight on the student him- or herself. One strong point that is made is that to some extent we are all mentally lazy. In the final section the student is to think about what mental activities will be the most important to him or her ten years hence.

Creative Thinking Skill to Be Developed: Looking from a Different Perspective

Some authorities term the creative thinking activity called for in this unit *analogizing*. It has proved to be a useful technique in many different problem-solving situations; analogizing usually is a fascinating and productive exercise when enough energy is invested in it. It would be safe to assume that some of your students aren't enthusiastic about activities such as analogizing, but we have tried to make the exercise more interesting by using the metaphor of the mind as an athlete.

Preparing for the Unit

There are many obvious occasions when an incident can set the stage for this unit—a just-completed game or an actual track meet, a discussion of the place of athletics in schools, a discussion of whether athletes are generally academic embarrassments to their schools at the college level, and other discussions about athletic and academic achievement.

Presenting the Unit

You may have students who point out, quite correctly, that there is a good deal of mental activity involved in athletic contests. Everything in sports is obviously not a matter of unthinking physical reaction. There are strategies in all sports, in some more so (as in tennis) and in some less so (as in pitching horseshoes).

Ordinarily, in these units the first section presents a good opportunity to kick around an idea or two. That may be particularly true of "Tracking the Mind." The two questions dealing with hopscotch and leapfrog can be discussed to whatever length you and the class take them, and then you can give your students the task of completing the remainder of the unit, including writing about what will be required of them intellectually ten years from now.

The footnote at the end of the first page of the unit brings up the topic of puns. There are people who can't resist punning. The headline writers of some newspapers seem to be striving continually for a pun. In a magnificent feat of combining puns and a mixed metaphor, one headline writer came up with "Stars come out as Clinton era dawns" after Bill Clinton's 1993 inaugural ball. And, admittedly, the title of this unit is a weak pun.

13 Tracking the Mind

1. We often hear the mind's being compared to a muscle—if you don't use it, it wastes away. Vigorous exercise of the mind is frequently thought of in terms of athletics. For example, a discussion in which ideas are batted back and forth can be likened to a tennis match.

What kind of mental activity can be compared to an individual playing hopscotch?

What about leapfrog?

2. If you thought of a track meet for the mind exclusively, a number of mental activities might be brought into play.* One of the events in a big track meet is actually comprised of ten events—the decathlon. What mental activities are suggested by the

hundred-yard dash?

high hurdles?

*Pun intended. What athletic event is comparable to contriving a pun?

pole vault?

1500-meter run?

discus?

shot put?

long jump?

400-meter sprint?

high jump?

javelin?

3. People might debate whether the pole vault requires more skills than running the quarter mile, and they might also argue about whether it is more difficult to write an essay or solve a mathematical problem. Certain physical and mental abilities are easy for some people and difficult for others.

Tracking the Mind *(continued)*

Which of the mental activities you assigned to the decathlon events is easiest for you? Tell why it is easy for you, and in doing so ask yourself if it is because that mental activity is one of your natural strengths or whether it is one that doesn't take much effort.

4. Now let's project into your future. Will that mental activity still be easy for you ten years from now? Will you be depending upon that mental activity as much or more when you are ten years older?

14
Couplets

An Invitation to Write Rhymed Verse

Overview

Following an introductory paragraph about pairs of words that rhyme, the unit engages your students in a game in which two words (an adjective modifying a noun) can be translated into a rhyming pair of words ("wet hobo" = "damp tramp"). Then the process is reversed and your students are asked to supply the nonrhyming pairs of words for seven rhyming pairs. From that point, they are asked to produce three pairs of rhyming words about the future. Finally, they are invited to compose couplets inspired by one of the rhymes about space.

Creative Thinking Skill to Be Developed: Being Original

Until they arrive at the third level, your students won't be doing much creative thinking in this unit. At that point, and in the writing activity, they will have to stretch their minds a little. Writing couplets in this case requires considerable original thinking because the couplets are supposed to be inspired by one of the three pairs of rhyming words about the future.

Preparing for the Unit

The game that opens the unit is sometimes called "Hinky Pinky." We've changed it slightly, but it is simply a rhyming activity. The best time to present the exercise is when your students are studying rhyming verse forms or when the topic of rhyme occurs in a discussion of writing. One shouldn't underestimate the importance of rhyme as an attention-getting and satisfying device. It gives feelings of completion and unity that are hard to obtain with other literary devices. On the other hand, this is not a really serious unit in the sense of developing important writing skills. It can be administered as a change of pace or as an introduction to the study of verse forms such as the couplet, especially if your class is reading the poetry of Pope or Dryden.

Presenting the Unit

The unit begins with challenging the student to come up with rhyming pairs of words for two words that are synonymous with each of the rhyming pairs. Although we would prefer that you first try to produce the seven rhymes yourself, these are some possible answers:

Wet hobo—damp tramp

Small library—book nook

Elated father—happy pappy, glad dad

Clever jogging—cunning running

Scholastic regulation—school rule

Obstreperous juvenile—wild child

Your students may well come up with different answers, and, as long as the answers rhyme and are close in meaning to the two unrhymed words, the responses are legitimate.

The second-level activity reverses the procedure, asking for synonymous pairs of words that go with the given rhymed words. Although it may not be more difficult for your students, it is generally harder to find just two words for a rhymed pair than the other way around.

At the third level, your students are asked to produce three hinky pinkies about the future. This is probably the most challenging task of the first three levels because there are no cues to work from, only the example of "Space Race."

The Writing Assignment

Having tried to produce pairs of words, your students are then invited to produce pairs of lines—in other words, couplets. Because of all the rhyming that they have done at the first two levels, your students should be in the proper frame of mind to write couplets about the future.

The couplet is a very old type of verse. Its classic metric form is iambic pentameter, but you probably won't want to worry your students about meter if you are simply trying to encourage them to do some writing. We hope that the rhyming game will get them in the mood to try their hands at writing rhymed verse.

The example of a four-line stanza we offer as a model shouldn't be taken as exemplary in any way. You can use more legitimate couplets if you think it advisable to do so. The "Space Race" verse was chosen more because it won't intimidate your students than for any possible poetic qualities. There is often a problem in offering young people an excellent model that they can't hope to match. Frequently they give up before really trying. In the instance of "Space Race," they should do much better.

14 Couplets

1\. Merchants and their advertisers like to use catchy words that rhyme. For example, for many years Piggly Wiggly was one of the biggest grocery chains in the country. Its name may have had something to do with its success. Rhymes are also used in the entertainment business, where slo-mo, hi-fi, and sci-fi are terms in common usage. Hanky-panky has been a popular expression for quite a while, and perhaps it will survive because of its catchiness.

A little game that is enjoyable to play is the one where you give a pair of words and someone tries to guess what rhyming pair of words are synonymous with the two words. To illustrate, if your friend says "unhappy father," you say "sad dad." Sometimes the pairs are pretty easy, but they can be tough too. Here are few of both kinds. Let's see how well you can do.

What two words describe a(n)

Wet hobo?

Small library?

Elated father?

Clever jogging?

Scholastic regulation?

Obstreperous juvenile?

Couplets *(continued)*

2. Let's reverse the process and give you the rhyming pair of words.

Can you come up with two synonyms for

Pay day?

Back pack?

Missed fist?

Funny bunny?

Fender bender?

Tearful earful?

Free tree?

Can you think of a rhyming pair that is synonymous with another rhyming pair (for example, an unhappy pappy is a sad dad)?

3. Let's go one step further.

Can you think of rhymes that are about things that might happen in the future? (An example would be "space race.") See if you can come up with at least three.

Couplets *(continued)*

4. Now take one of your rhymes about the future and make it into a rhyming verse. It would be appropriate if the type of verse is the couplet, which has two lines that rhyme. Write two couplets to the stanza so that your stanzas will be four lines long. Your couplets can be lighthearted or serious. Here is an example of one that isn't too serious:

Space Race
Here in this module in my pressurized suit,
Though cramped and wet, I don't give a hoot,
Because if I beat them all to far-off Riz
They'll see that as a racer I'm one big whiz!

Here is some space for working out your rhyming lines about the future. Try to write at least two stanzas.

15
Hear Here!

An Invitation to Write an Advertisement

Overview

"Hear Here!" was a real ad. We didn't make it up. Copywriters for advertising agencies rely upon an assortment of tricks. They are fond of puns, alliteration, catch phrases, and vivid metaphors. Their affection for the language and for humor usually shines through their work. The other homonym pairs given in this unit are original with us (as far as we know), and that fact may attest to our proclivity for attempting to put humor in writing.

In the first section of the unit the student only has to explain "Hear Here!" and "Fair Fare." An old theory regarding the presentation of materials to students is to have the easiest come first. That is the strategy employed in this unit.

The second section is a little more difficult but not much more. In that part, the student does some more explaining of homonym pairs. There's a bit more of a challenge in the third section, a guessing game in which the student tries to identify seven pairs of homonyms from the descriptions given (very similar to the kind of guessing done in a crossword puzzle). In the fourth section, we ask the student to come up with five pairs of homonyms that can make a statement.

Finally, we invite the student to write an ad with a heading of homonyms. We suggest that the copy run to no more than sixty words, but many fewer should be the norm. Our assumption is that all of your students will be quite familiar with newspaper and magazine ads, but it would be a good idea to have a few distinctive ones on hand when you administer this unit.

Preparing for the Unit

The logical tie-in with this unit is a discussion of advertising. Since we are bombarded constantly with electronic and print ads, every one of your students is an expert about advertising. Because of television, each has probably spent thousands of hours watching and listening to pitches about a multitude of products. How much time your students spend reading ads in magazines, newspapers, and catalogues would depend to a great extent upon their socioeconomic situations and the locality of your school.

Presenting the Unit

You may want to administer the first two parts of the unit orally to your class. A discussion of the questions concerning "Hear Here!" and "Fair Fare" should sufficiently warm up your students so that the five pairs to be explained in the second section pose no difficulties. We recommend that the third part be tackled by your students individually. It may be that they will want to share their answers or check to see if their answers agree with those of their classmates. You can handle the sharing in any way you like. And that goes, of course, for the entire unit—you can modify parts or throw parts out entirely.

A couple of words we use, proboscis and ursine, will probably be absent in the vocabularies of some of your students. Maybe we like to throw in an occasional word that requires a dictionary, but that wasn't our intention in this unit. We were just searching for synonyms to be used in the game.

15 Hear Here!

Being Original

1. This was the heading for a radio station's ad.

   What is meant by "Hear Here!"?

   What would someone carrying a placard reading "Fair Fare!" be protesting?

   In each case there are two homonyms placed together in such a way that a statement is made. Homonyms, as you know, are words that sound alike but are different in meaning and are usually spelled differently.

2. What situations do these pairs of homonyms describe?

   Whole Hole

   Sail Sale

   Pear Pair

   Wise Whys

   Stake Steak

Hear Here! *(continued)*

3. What pairs of homonyms fit these descriptions? Write just two words.

The sixty minutes that belong to us.

To illegally take a very strong metal.

Someone was victorious.

In a film, an American Indian reports, after putting his ear to the ground, that buffalo are coming.

A professional's writing (not poetry).

Recognizes a proboscis.

An ursine adult loses its fur because of a disease.

4. Can you come up with five pairs of homonyms like the ones above?

Write your homonyms in the space below. Then, if you'd like, give them to one or more of your classmates and find out how difficult the homonyms are.

Hear Here! *(continued)*

5. Why don't you try your hand at writing an ad like "Hear Here!" with a pair of homonyms? After coming up with a heading, write the rest of the advertisement, using no more than sixty words, about a product that hasn't yet come on the market. Sketch in any photographs or drawings where they might be appropriately placed.

   Use the space below for roughing in your ad using homonyms.

16
A Man and a Butterfly

An Invitation to Write a News Story

Overview

The unit starts off with the entire feature story from a midwestern newspaper of a man who has a pet butterfly. Your students are asked a few questions about Raymond and his butterfly (which is really a moth), and then they are asked more questions about the relationships, now and in the future, between humans and animals. Finally, they are invited to write a newspaper article of the feature story type about our changing relationships with animals.

Creative Thinking Skill to Be Developed: Being Original

As is the case with many of these units, in "A Man and a Butterfly" your students are asked to think critically before being invited to think creatively. The two kinds of thinking, we should add, are certainly not incompatible. However, since by far the greatest attention in schools is given to critical thinking, creative thinking is often pushed aside or even pooh-poohed. When people are being creative they have to analyze, establish criteria, and make judgments—often simultaneously—as they try to produce things that are original.

Preparing for the Unit

This unit features a news story of the kind that has been called "human interest." The theme of the unit, as well as of the article, is the relationships between human beings and animals. If your students are reading any of the countless books that have been written about our relationships with animals, you will have an excellent tie-in with this unit.

The issues raised in this unit are very important ones. There could be several students in your classes who are interested in saving the whales and other endangered species. These young people will probably react strongly to the questions of the unit, and they can also be sources of information for their classmates. A discussion about the efforts of a conservation group would be an excellent way to lead into this unit and its poignant story of a little man and a butterfly.

Presenting the Unit

As is the case with most of the units of *What Next?* this unit has three levels of involvement for the student. The first level, which serves as a warm-up and introduction to the topic at hand, is comprised of the news article and two questions that are designed to induce the student to think a little more deeply about the story. At the second level, the student is first asked to reflect upon our history of living on Earth with other members of the "animal kingdom" and then to contemplate what changes will be wrought in the many continuing sagas of humans and their fellow animals.

Because the article that starts the unit is an effective warm-up, this is the type of unit that can be administered successfully with or without your leading an introductory discussion. However, the unit probably will benefit tremendously from one or more discussions with the entire class.

The Writing Assignment

At the third level of student involvement, the invitation is given to write a similar news article, to be published in the future, about a changing situation between human beings and animals. In recent years, there have been a number of changes in our attitudes about animals. To name just two, we no longer feel that we can ignore what happens to animal and plant life when we change the environment; and we also realize that exploitation of animals for our food, comfort, and entertainment can lead to the extinction of species, thus creating ecological imbalances that ultimately hurt humankind.

In quite another vein, the 1980s witnessed a rather widespread recognition of the psychotherapeutic value of pets such as cats and dogs. They are being used widely—with excellent results—with elderly people, certain types of emotionally disturbed children and adults, and other groups. Some studies have indicated that stroking and talking with a pet reduces high blood pressure. The fundamental question, however, is whether human beings have the right to exterminate other animals, whether purposely or capriciously.

16 A Man and a Butterfly

1. The article below appeared in a midwestern newspaper several years ago.

Man and the Butterfly:

Get an Earful of This!

by Carl Hennemann, Staff Writer

Let me tell you, patrons of the Brass Rail looked a second time when Raymond and his friend walked in Tuesday afternoon.

Some of the customers of the bar at 225 W. Seventh St. blamed it on the heat; others weren't sure the explanation was so simple.

But habitues of the establishment turned back to their glasses unworried. They are familiar with Raymond Cleveland's pet butterfly.

Cleveland, a bachelor, is 48 and lives at 24 Wilkin St. He works as a helper on a rubbish-hauling truck owned and driven by Erby Campeau, 229 Sherman St.

The saga of the butterfly began one day last month. It had started out to be just another day for the rubbish haulers, but everything changed when Erby and Raymond stopped in the 900 block on Grand Ave.

The butterfly flew into the cab of the truck and perched on Raymond's ear.

It was the beginning of a strange relationship. The butterfly likes quiet, little Raymond and spurns big, beefy Erby. It especially likes Raymond's ears.

It spends the nights in the truck, but in the morning, when Raymond gets into the truck, it flutters onto his right ear and clings there. Ray, in his quiet way, likes this too.

[For the record, the butterfly actually is a cecropia moth, one of the largest and most colorful moths found in Minnesota. However, the trash haulers and their friends considered it a butterfly, so we will also.]

"It won't go to anybody but Raymond," Erby explains in a loud voice. "What do you feed butterflies? I tried to give this one water and potato chips."

A reporter was summoned to the Brass Rail to get an eyeful of this sweet friendship between the beautiful butterfly and Raymond.

Raymond was sitting rigidly in a booth, close to the wall. He stared ahead glassy-eyed and his long, thin neck was stiff as a fence post. His friend was on his ear, and Raymond didn't move a muscle to cause it any discomfort.

"What's its name?" the reporter asked, trying to think up a few fast questions.

Erby took over. "We never gave it a name, didn't know how long it would last!" he shouted. "Show him the butterfly!"

Raymond carefully took the butterfly off his ear and put it on the table. It fluttered and crawled back to Raymond's hand and tried to crawl up his arm toward his ear.

"Why should it prefer Raymond?" the reporter asked.

"Because Raymond smells good to the butterfly," someone said.

Raymond says little, just sits stiffly, the moth neatly perched.

Its wings are a little shabby after its month on Raymond's ear, and the red, mossy fur between its wings a little dusty from much handling.

Moths are short-lived so the saga of Raymond and his butterfly might end any day now.

But for Raymond, lonely man, it has been a strange and wonderful friendship.

A Man and a Butterfly *(continued)*

If you had been the reporter, what other questions would you have asked Raymond and Erby?

Does the reporter exhibit any prejudices that he might have in this article? Explain.

Do you have any ideas as to why the butterfly (moth) preferred Raymond to Erby?

2. People have used animals for food, transportation, and companionship since the beginning of our time on Earth. Human beings have also been the victims of animals occasionally, but infinitely more animals have been victimized by human beings.

Have our relationships with animals changed appreciably over the millennia? If so, in what ways have they changed?

A Man and a Butterfly *(continued)*

Are any of the relationships changing now? If so, will they change even more in the future? How will they change?

Which group of animals will probably be changed most among mammals, insects, birds, reptiles, marine life, and micro-organisms? Why do you think so?

A Man and a Butterfly *(continued)*

3. Why don't you write a news article that describes the changing relationships between humankind and one group of animals?

You can use the space below to sketch out your ideas for the news article.

17
Feeling Colorful

An Invitation to Write a Quintet

Overview

The opening section deals with associating colors with feelings, which leads your students to supplying four colors, one each to go with pride, delight, boredom, and resentment, and then four feelings or emotions to go with four colors. The second section offers a bit more challenge by asking students to think of three combinations of feelings and colors connected by the word "without." From linking emotions and colors, your students are invited to write a quintet that features an emotion.

Creative Thinking Skill to Be Developed: Being Original

Right from the start of this unit your students are asked to think originally, first in composing word combinations featuring the connective "with" and then in coming up with word combinations featuring "without." The unit culminates in an invitation to write a quintet, a verse form that has a set pattern of syllables for its five lines. The quintet may be a test of both your students' grasp of versifying and of their ingenuity in using a limited number of words to convey an emotion.

Preparing for the Unit

As with other units in this idea book, "Feeling Colorful" deals with the everyday expressions that people use (and sometimes overuse) to communicate vividly to others. As the title indicates, the expressions to be examined in this unit can be presented whenever you feel the oral and/or written language of your students is too dependent upon clichés. If yours is a class of average teenagers, you'll be able to use this exercise throughout the year.

All of us—not only young people—are very susceptible to imitating the speech mannerisms of others. But there is little teachers can do about upgrading the language of those not in school. A personal crusade to eliminate a verbal crutch such as "you know" or to get people to have their subjects agree with their verb forms is more an exercise in futility than anything else. It is next to impossible to eradicate unattractive verbal mannerisms in young people too, but teachers can make students more self-critical of their writing, because by its nature writing is not transitory but can be examined and changed.

Presenting the Unit

The first part of the unit plunges the student right into the task of inventing new expressions that utilize words we use for colors. This activity presupposes that the student has a decent vocabulary of color words. That may not be the case, and so you might suggest that a dictionary, a thesaurus, and a reference book containing information about color be used as aids in devising new "colorful expressions." One of our prime objectives in writing these units is to encourage learning of all kinds.

At the second level, the student is to produce more colorful expressions. In contrast to the first set, the three expressions to be invented have the connective "without" instead of "with." The examples given are "blue without you" and "magenta without misery." You probably can think of others if your students need additional cuing.

The Writing Assignment

We hope that when the student arrives at the third level he or she has given enough thought to emotions that it won't be difficult to write a quintet about an emotion. As we point out in the exercise, however, producing a quintet forces a discipline upon the writer. Quintets have lines of 3, 5, 7, 9, and 3 syllables, which doesn't permit many words to be used.

The example of a quintet offered the student in the unit uses one color (grey). Perhaps one of the "colorful expressions" invented at the first or second level could serve the student well in one of the lines. It is more important, however, that a degree of freshness be exhibited by the student in writing about an emotion.

17 Feeling Colorful

1. We frequently associate a color with a particular emotion that someone is feeling. For example, you have often heard people described as being "green with envy," "blue with sadness," and "purple with rage." The names of colors add a pictorial quality to our descriptions of people. In some cases there is a good reason for the color that is associated with the emotion. There is some physiological basis for saying that someone is "purple with rage," since that color communicates a good deal about blood vessels, blood pressure, respiration, and the like, of people who are terribly angry. There is also a psychological basis since purple is one of the most intense colors in the spectrum and rage is one of the most intense emotions. On the other hand, it becomes a little tiring always to hear of a person as being *green* with envy. Why can't she or he become another color, such as mauve or brown? Why can't we find some other colorful expression to describe emotional people? What about "pink with expectation" (something like "bursting with curiosity") or "orange with frustration"?

You can probably think of some interesting colors to accompany a set of feelings.

Begin with filling in the blanks for these:

____________________ with pride
____________________ with boredom
____________________ with delight
____________________ with resentment

Now reverse the process. Fill in an *emotion* for these colors:

turquoise with ____________________
brown with ______________________
crimson with ____________________
yellow with ______________________
(don't use cowardice)

Feeling Colorful *(continued)*

2. You might even be able to think of a color that can be used when something is lacking, as "blue without you" or "magenta without misery." You probably can think of better combinations.

_______________ without _______________
_______________ without _______________
_______________ without _______________

3. There is no need to mention how important emotions are. We know that they color all of the events of our lives. Poets try to capture the feelings that most of us have experienced. The poets attempt to use words in such a way that we can see another aspect of a common experience—we see it in greater depth or from a different perspective.

The *quintet* is one form of poetry that requires writers to be very economical with words as they try to express their views of the world. The syllabic pattern is similar to the schemes for haiku and cinquains, with lines of 3, 5, 7, 9, and 3 syllables. Here is an example of a rather serious quintet:

Where There's Life

Frail grey friend,
Where's your rosy glow?
Each day you grow more fragile,
Less a reality, more a ghost
—Are you Hope?

Feeling Colorful *(continued)*

Now you can try your hand at composing a quintet. You might use some of the ideas you listed in the activity about emotions and colors to get yourself started.

Use the space below to write your quintet. It's a good plan to write down the phrases and words as they come to you, and then you can work on arranging them meaningfully into the pattern of the verse.

18
Music

An Invitation to Write a Cinquain

Overview

The first two parts of the unit deal with the topic of music. After a discussion of the various uses of music, the student is asked to explain forced analogies of music and seven disparate subjects. This activity leads in to an invitation to write a cinquain.

Creative Thinking Skills to Be Developed: Seeing Relationships; Being Original

It is likely that your students will develop increased skill in seeing relationships as a result of completing this unit. If they take the forced analogies seriously, they will have to stretch their minds to see connections between music and a burglar and music and a mountain. (Do you see any connections?)

The likelihood of developing the skill of thinking in novel ways may be just as easily realized in this unit because cinquains are easy to write, and that characteristic allows the student to make associations without referring to what others have written. The structure, however, is restrictive, so there is some discipline required in sticking to the pattern.

Preparing for the Unit

Since the topic examined in the unit is music, there should be many opportunities to introduce it to your students. The idea of *using* music can be remarked upon because music is employed in a host of ways today to accomplish a very wide variety of objectives.

Presenting the Unit

The best way to prepare yourself for this unit (and most of the others in this book) is to do the activity yourself. In that way you can discover the unit's strengths and weaknesses, and you can also guess how it will go over with your students. The strategy used in this particular unit has been employed by the authors on many occasions. Analogizing is a natural way of leading in to cinquain writing, and that's how we have done it. Whether our experiences have been wildly successful or not doesn't make much difference to you and your students, but they work well for us.

A number of critical factors are involved in the administration of any activity such as "Music." You know the waters are largely uncharted, and so you know there is risk. Most children and adults find cinquains appealing, however, and so might your students.

One word of caution: Don't worry too much if your students don't adhere to the syllabic pattern of the cinquain. It's the idea that counts.

18 Music

1. If you asked various people what music means to them, you'd get a variety of answers. Some might respond that music means a lot to them, but others might not know what to say. Maybe if you ask, instead, what they use music for, the answers would be more specific. You could get answers such as enjoyment, dancing, marching, inspiration, escape, mood changing, excitement, comfort, celebrating, washing the dishes to, self-expression, writing poems to, painting to, and blocking out noises.

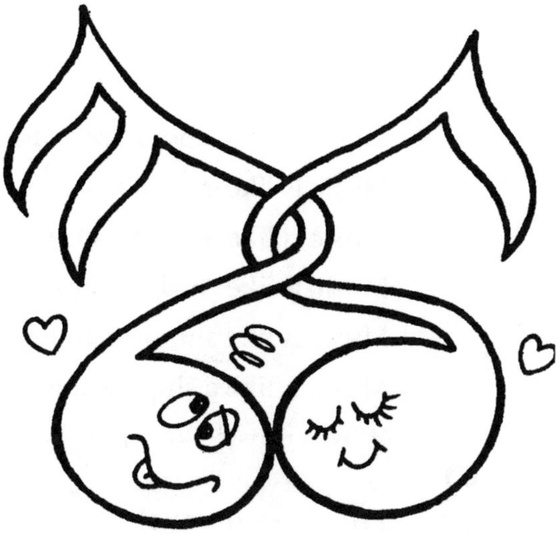

How would you answer if someone asked you what you use music for?

What daily activity is closest to music in its basic nature?

Why is it akin to music?

2. A famous song states, "A pretty girl is like a melody." What other analogies can we make with music? Try these:

Music is like a poem because ______________________________

Music is like a farm because ______________________________

Music is like a rainbow because ______________________________

Music is like April because ______________________________

Music is like a mountain because ______________________________

Music is like a ship because ______________________________

Why is music like a burglar? ______________________________

3. Look over the analogies you have just considered. Which of them interests you most?

Because verse contains allusion, metaphor, personification, and other figures of speech, the analogy you have just cited could serve you well in writing some verse. You might choose a form of verse such as the cinquain. The cinquain is relatively easy to compose because of its structure and brevity. It has just five lines, each longer than the one before, except for the last line. This is the scheme for a cinquain:

First line—two syllables, stating the subject
Second line—four syllables, describing the subject
Third line—six syllables, portraying action
Fourth line—eight syllables, conveying feeling
Fifth line—two syllables, another way of stating the subject.

Music *(continued)*

Writing cinquains is not difficult. You may want to write more than one.

19
Windless Sails

An Invitation to Write Humorous Dialogue

Overview

Your students are asked how they might react to five deflating experiences, and then they are invited to write some humorous dialogue based on one of those ego-puncturing experiences. Perhaps the five incidents will seem more frustrating and infuriating than amusing, but much of what we term humorous is of this type of experience.

Creative Thinking Skill to Be Developed: Being Original

Humor is difficult to communicate well in any kind of writing. The novice generally relies upon exaggeration, and his or her words frequently are simply far-fetched. Even the newspaper columns of professional writers often fall flat because there is too much exaggeration and not enough genuine humor in their work. Therefore, the verbal ingenuity called for in this unit is of a high order. We're asking your students to be original—and funny. It's not easy.

Preparing for the Unit

The concept used to initiate "Windless Sails" is deflation. As used in this unit, deflation means letting the air out of something, both literally and figuratively. The economic meaning of the term isn't used, but it could serve as a lead-in as well as could remarks about people being deflated after losing or being squelched. The squelching business, incidentally, will probably be the aspect of the unit that will appeal most to your students. "Put-downs" are popular (and unpopular) with teenagers, and the writing activities are entirely a matter of thinking how people can be put down. Accordingly, if that particular malady is manifested in the behavior of your students (and it is very probable that it is), this unit can be presented with the assurance that it will get emotional reactions.

Presenting the Unit

After an introduction or lead-in about deflating egos or squelching, you can present the unit to your students and let them go to it. We anticipate that there is nearly a total membership among the members of your classes of the "Wish I'd Said That" club. After being insulted, ignored, or humiliated, the natural feeling is to want to "get even." Here is a chance, if only in a writing exercise, to get rid of that unlovely but all-too-human feeling.

The exercise starts off with a discussion of the idea of deflation, that is, letting the air out of things. Journalists and other writers are fond of the word, and so your students will have relatively few problems responding to the questions about the consequences of letting air out of a basketball, a wind sock, a pair of lungs, a bicycle tube, a life raft, someone's high spirits, or a big ego. The last item leads into the second-level activity of coming up with well-chosen words for people who exhibit insulting behavior. We can imagine that a few of your students will work especially hard at this task.

The Writing Assignment

The writing activity evolves naturally from the conjuring up of withering, deflationary sentences. Your students are to select one of the situations for which they have written a rejoinder or put-down and expand it into a humorous dialogue. What constitutes humor for the student, however, may not be amusing to you. That modifier is important, nonetheless, because we don't want to encourage vicious or merely vengeful thinking. Accordingly, it might be a good idea for you to encourage a certain amount of good will on the part of your students before they get too carried away with themes of retribution. You will know just how to handle the assignment, of course, and the purpose here is to get the pencils moving.

The form of dialogue is simple enough if students know how to punctuate direct quotations. Some short stories are almost entirely dialogue, with very little description of the setting and characters. It takes practice to write effective dialogue, but the nature of this particular assignment should be motivating enough so that your students can imagine what might be said quite vividly.

19 Windless Sails

1. You can put air into any number of things, and you can let the air out of those things, too. Familiar objects such as car tires, balloons, footballs, soccer balls, and air mattresses are not useful unless they are inflated with air. What can happen when you let the air out of these:

A basketball?

A wind sock?

A pair of lungs?

A bicycle tube?

A life raft?

Someone's high spirits?

A big ego?

(Incidentally, at one time a disagreeable or dull date was called a "flat tire," in other words, a keen disappointment or small disaster.) So, when we deflate something, we drastically reduce its usefulness.

2. At times, though, it is fun to "burst someone's balloon" or "take the wind out of someone's sails," especially if he or she is pompous or conceited. In looking to your future, you may have thought of situations in which you could encounter someone's puffery, pomposity, or inflated ego. Have you thought of how you might handle those situations? Imagine that a few of these experiences will actually happen to you, and then tell how you will react to each one. What will you do if

A prospective employer keeps you waiting in an outer office for two hours in order to impress you with how busy and important he is and how insignificant you are?

An acquaintance tells you, for thirty-five minutes, about how all the boys or girls are crazy about her or him?

You are invited to a party and one of the guests talks only to the person you are with, never acknowledging your presence, because he or she believes your companion is intellectually capable of understanding the conversation and you aren't?

A teacher forgets two consecutive appointments with you because he can't seem to remember such minor details when he's so busy with committee work?

Windless Sails *(continued)*

A waiter in a fancy restaurant ignores your table until you are about to leave and then gives you some curt, impolite answers to your questions about the menu selections?

3. Why don't you take one of these situations and write some humorous dialogue about what might transpire? Everyone has had the experience of thinking of the perfect retort *after* it is too late—the time for delivering the rejoinder has long since passed. But in this exercise, you'll have a chance to think of your comebacks and put-downs *before* these situations arise.

Use the space below to sketch your ideas for the humorous exchanges. Use additional paper as necessary!

20
Impressions

An Invitation to Write Verse

Overview

"Impressions" is designed to encourage your students to be more aware of everyday phenomena. They are first asked to make some word associations with a variety of words (from "fog" to "an old tire"). Then your students are encouraged to reflect upon things that make them marvel, jotting down adjectives appropriate for the marvelous items about which they have thought. Finally, they are asked to put their thinking into a form of verse.

Creative Thinking Skill to Be Developed: Being Original

It is important to give credit to original ideas in writing. We have found that students who are rewarded for originality in their writing, compared with their classmates who are rewarded for correctness, write longer, more original, and more interesting stories (Torrance and Myers 1970).

Preparing for and Presenting the Unit

The theme of this unit is nearly identical to the one in Rachel Carson's *A Sense of Wonder.* If you have access to the book, you'll find that any number of her sentences might be quoted to set the proper mood for this unit.

"Impressions" is one of those classroom activities that works especially well if it is introduced by your calling attention to an object of some kind and displaying it to your students. The object can be ordinary, such as a peanut or an acorn; or it can be remarkable in some way, perhaps a chambered nautilus or a coconut. Whatever object you use, call attention to its amazing properties. The coconut, for instance, was first given that name because it reminded the Portuguese of a monkey, probably suggested by the hairy surface and the three dots on the shell.* (Why *does* a coconut have those three marks?) The shape, color and cap of an acorn, as commonplace as it is, are remarkable too. You can call attention to the marvelous features of any object that your students see—but do not particularly notice—in their everyday world.

The Writing Assignment

The invitation to write a poem should be considered optional for some groups of students. A good deal of groundwork usually has to be laid before an entire class will take on a poetry writing assignment willingly, but many teachers are able to obtain a very high degree of participation in a writing exercise such as the one proposed in this unit. No particular form of verse is mentioned in the unit, and our recommendation to you is that you mention a relatively easy form (perhaps one that has been mastered in previous lessons) and then allow your students to adopt any form that seems appropriate to them.

Reference

Carson, Rachel. *A Sense of Wonder.* New York: Harper & Row, 1987.

Torrance, E. Paul, and Robert E. Myers. *Creative Learning and Teaching.* New York: Harper, 1970.

*The Portuguese word for monkey is "cocos."

20 Impressions

1. When you see a tortoise or read about one, the ideas of durability, age, slowness, or protection may come to your mind. What ideas come to your mind when you think of these things?

fog

ice cream

a snowflake

a pair of scissors

an ocean

a postage stamp

an ant

a broken window

Impressions *(continued)*

a mushroom

an eyelash

a discarded doll

a handkerchief

confetti

a dragonfly

an old tire

2. What things in life always cause you to marvel every time they are brought to your attention?

List your "marvelous" things in the space below.

Impressions *(continued)*

3. Can you think of some good adjectives to describe the things you believe to be particularly wonderful? Search your mind (or the dictionary) for adjectives that capture the essence and the flavor of the things they describe.

MARVELOUS THINGS **ADJECTIVES**

Impressions *(continued)*

4. If you would like to do some more thinking about any of the "wonders of life" that you have described on the previous page, why don't you put your thoughts into poetic form? Poetry is one of the most powerful means we have of expressing life's truths, partly because it represents a distillation of our emotions and discoveries.

   Use the space below to work out ideas for your "wonders of life" poem.

21
Up and Out

An Invitation to Write a Tall Tale

Overview

"Up and Out" challenges the student to explore the notion of explosions. After we give the student a brief introduction of the concept, he or she is asked to think of the consequences of the blowing up of an ego, a building, an excuse, a piece of gossip, and a disposition. Obviously some of these explosions are not entirely physical, but the idea is to have the student think metaphorically in examining the notion of something getting bigger in a hurry.

The second section consists of an open-ended question about blow-ups at home or school. It is likely that the student will interpret the term metaphorically rather than literally.

In the final section of the unit, the student is invited to write a tall tale, a story that is "blown up." A few words about the nature of the tall tale genre are given, and then the student is free to respond in any way that appeals to her or him.

Creative Thinking Skill to Be Developed: Being Original

It is quite easy to imagine that we are developing creative thinking when we ask young people to write fiction. Unless they deliberately copy something written by someone else or steal ideas from others, writing fiction should be, *ipso facto,* an exercise in thinking creatively. But professional writers derive their ideas from other writers, so it is difficult to determine how truly original any creative writing—especially the productions of students—is. We know a good percentage of students' fiction derives from television programs. The students who tend to be lazy will seize upon ideas presented more or less ready-made for them by television.

How you counteract this inclination to "borrow" ideas from others will in part determine how successful your fiction writing activity will be. Perhaps just mentioning that they should rely principally upon their own imaginations rather than upon the talents of television writers will do the trick.

Preparing for the Unit

Without exception, any activity whose principal *raison d'etre* is to promote creative thinking should be undertaken in an atmosphere conducive to freeing the imagination, and that means a situation that is tolerant of differences in people's ideas and one in which the individual feels free to experiment and allow one idea to lead to another naturally. Any distraction will take a toll of the individual's creative energies, and negative thoughts are likely to undercut her or his efforts to think creatively.

How you prepare your students for an activity involving them in writing tall tales will be crucial to their success in the endeavor. It may be that the topic of tall tales has come up in a discussion or perhaps as a lesson or unit of the language arts curriculum. If so, "Up and Out" can capitalize upon the interest generated by the discussion or lesson.

It is best not to interrupt your students with additional instructions, advice, or admonitions once they are embarked on the writing journey. On the other hand, they should feel perfectly safe in consulting you about anything related to their stories during the writing activity.

Presenting the Unit

It might be a good idea to have a general discussion with your class about explosions before having your students tackle the writing assignment. There can be a certain amount of healthy humor engendered in contemplating the various explosions suggested in the first section of the unit.

You may or may not want to engage your students in an open discussion of the problems arising from explosions at home and at school. Assuredly the questions can elicit some very emotional responses, so you may elect only to encourage a discussion of the relatively less volatile questions in the first section. The limits to your role in exploring topics such as violence in the home are determined by factors that differ from school to school and from teacher to teacher.

21 Up and Out

1. You are quite familiar with things getting blown up, aren't you? Balloons get blown up. Photographs get blown up. Sometimes chemistry sets get blown up. It often happens when stories get passed along from one person to another. There is a tendency in all of us to make the story "a little bit better." This kind of blowing up is called exaggerating.

What happens when these things are blown up?

An ego?

A building?

An excuse?

Gossip?

A disposition?

2. What things have you seen blown up at home or at school recently? What happened?

   Describe at least two of the things you have seen blown up and the effects.

3. Think of an experience that you or one of your friends might have thirty years from now, and then write a tall tale about it. Start with just a small amount of exaggeration, and then make the tale more and more far-fetched as you go along. Reach a point in your tale when one more piece of exaggeration will solve a problem or provide a big laugh.

   Remember that a tall tale is like a regular story except that the actions and abilities of some of the characters and the dimensions of things are far beyond our usual expectations. So there has to be a story line, that is, a beginning, build-up, climax, and ending.

Up and Out *(continued)*

Sketch out your ideas and the outline of the plot for your tall tale in the space below.

22
Guilt

An Invitation to Predict How Future Guilt Will Be Handled

Overview

This unit is really about guilt—all kinds of guilt. In the first part your students are asked to think of actions that can be taken to assuage guilt feelings after the commission of a variety of sins, some large and a few not so big. All of the actions described, however, are serious enough to bother a person's conscience for some time. In the second part of the unit your students are asked which of the ten sins could first be forgotten by someone who had taken the proper steps to make amends.

Projecting themselves into situations involving cheating, discrimination, and shoplifting, your students, in the last part, predict how those behaviors will be dealt with thirty years from now. Will society regard all of them in the same way they are regarded now?

Creative Thinking Skill to Be Developed: Being Sensitive and Aware

It's a fairly good guess that there will be a variety of reactions to this unit. Even though the misbehaviors described range from a punishable crime to an indiscretion, each misdeed can lead to a chain of events, all of them disagreeable. The seriousness with which each misbehavior is taken will probably vary widely from student to student. Conceivably, there are young people in your class who are not fully aware of the ramifications of actions such as boasting dishonestly or discriminating against people because of their religious convictions. We hope that they can be sensitized to the problems that arise because of thoughtless as well as dishonest behavior.

Preparing for the Unit

This unit is about ethics, a subject that over recent years has been given ever-increasing attention nationally. Any occasion at school, in the community, or in the world at large that reveals people acting unethically will provide an excellent lead-in to the unit. Unfortunately, there are usually plenty of instances where unethical conduct becomes an issue, and you can probably lead in with one on almost any school day of the year.

Presenting the Unit

If your students aren't sick and tired of discussing morals and ethics, this unit could take up a lot of time. It's loaded with issues that bear upon the everyday lives of your students. We recommend that the first part be undertaken as a general discussion. If there are any cynics among your students, they may make themselves known in the discussion. Each student should respond to the remainder of the unit alone.

When your students reach the last part of the unit, they will have an opportunity to find out for themselves whether they are optimistic or pessimistic about how people are going to deal with the basic problems of living together. Will anything be different thirty years from now? None of us knows, but it's one of the most important questions that can be asked.

22 Guilt

1. Although probably an exaggeration, it has often been said that we are a "guilt-ridden" society. Certainly there is a good deal of emphasis upon removing guilt feelings nowadays, especially by counselors, clerics, and writers giving advice in periodicals. But how do we acquire feelings of guilt? We can experience them because of something we have done, because of something we have not done, or because of something someone else has or hasn't done. Unfortunately, we can experience genuine feelings of guilt when someone, or a group of people with whom we identify, does or does not take action. No wonder it is easy to feel guilty.

Without asking you if you have had feelings of guilt recently, we'd like to ask you what might be done to remove guilty feelings after these events have taken place. In other words, what should the "guilty party" do to feel less guilty?

Bragging about something you really didn't do.

Yelling at someone you love when that person shouldn't have been yelled at.

Cheating on a test.

Taking money from a parent's pocketbook or wallet.

Shoplifting.

Telling your parents that you are going out to do one thing and then doing something else that they don't approve of.

Participating with a group of friends in excluding someone from your group because of the person's religion.

Participating with a group of friends in excluding someone from your group because of the person's race.

Being part of a prank that injured an elderly person.

Getting overheard saying something uncomplimentary about an acquaintance, whose feelings were terribly hurt.

2. Some people are never able to get over their guilt feelings. They remember what they did wrong all of their lives. Others forget or forgive themselves.

Which of the ten guilt experiences described in section 1 are likely to be forgotten after the person has taken action to remove the guilt from his or her conscience? Tell why you think so.

3. Let's take three of those guilt-producing events and predict how they might be regarded by society thirty years from now.

How will cheating in school be handled?

How will excluding someone from a group because of race be dealt with?

How will shoplifting be dealt with?

Now tell whether you think the persons involved in those three actions will feel more, or less, guilty thirty years from now than they do today.

4. You might be interested to know that in Tibetan there is no word for guilt. The concept is foreign to Tibetans.

Comment on how a culture that does not have a word for guilt might be different from your own.

23
Vanity

An Invitation to Write a Dialogue

Overview

The unit's three parts involve your students in three related activities. First, after an introduction to the idea of associating people with numbers, there is a section in which your students are asked to guess about the personalities of the owners of seven quite different vehicles bearing vanity license plates. Then they are asked to think of a possible system of identification for vehicles in the future that differs from the one in use now. Finally, your students are invited to write a dialogue for three of the people they have described in the first section.

Creative Thinking Skills to Be Developed: Seeing Relationships; Being Original

Associating names, faces, numbers, backgrounds, and occupations is an activity most of us do naturally. When we make associations purposefully, however, some mental effort is involved. Deliberate associations are made by writers, of course, as they contrive their plots. We presume that the associations made by your students in the first part of the unit will help them in writing a dialogue for three of their hypothetical drivers.

Preparing for the Unit

You might introduce this unit by asking your students if any members of their families own cars with vanity plates. If the answer is yes, you can ask why those particular combinations of letters and numbers were chosen. The reasons for composing some vanity plates are genuinely fascinating. People are often making a statement in requesting a certain vanity plate, but there are others who want a combination that is easy to remember (a problem for some of us). A discussion of vanity plates should set up the unit in a way that will ensure a high level of interest in all three of its parts.

Presenting the Unit

After the introductory discussion of vanity plates, you might be well advised to let your students individually go ahead with the unit itself. A number of "cute" remarks made aloud could inhibit the imaginations of less outgoing students, so we recommend that a discussion of the personalities of "UR A QT," "SEE YA," and the others be postponed until after your students have completed the writing activity at the end.

23 Vanity

1. A former professional football coach enjoys taking a number, for example, 14, and telling what a player with that number might be like. "Fourteen" in the numbering system used in collegiate and professional football can be used only by a quarterback (10 through 19 are reserved for quarterbacks). The coach, through many years of associating players and numbers, can rattle off something about the physical characteristics, home territory, general proclivities, weaknesses, and so on, of "Ole 14."

Have you ever noticed a vanity plate and wondered what kind of person the owner of the car really is? Sometimes it is obvious from a glance at the driver, but the driver isn't necessarily the owner of the vehicle. Here are some license plates noted during the past several months. What do you think the owners of the vehicles are like? You might consider these options:

male or female
age
preference in clothing
occupation
physical characteristics
personality

License Plates on These Cars

MY XS *(red RX7 Turbo II Mazda)*

UR A QT *(white RS V8 Camaro)*

TUBA *(blue Dynasty LE Dodge)*

YEE HAW *(white Jeep Cherokee 4x4)*

SEE YA *(yellow 914 Porsche)*

GO 22 *(blue CRX si Honda)*

BIGO 2 *(green Lumina APV van)*

2. Let's suppose that it is some time in the future and license plates are no longer used.

What other device or system could be used to identify cars and their owners?

Vanity *(continued)*

3. Take three of the people you have described and have them converse with one another. You can take your cues from the ways you have described them in deciding what they will talk about and how they will react to one another's words.

Write your conversation in the space below.

24
Heroism

An Invitation to Write a Scene in the Life of a Future Hero

Overview

The unit begins with an account of an act of heroism, followed by a brief discussion of heroism. Your students are then asked to predict who might be likely heroes for seven fields of endeavor thirty years hence. After thinking about who could qualify as heroes in those various fields, they are asked to select one and write about that hero-to-be. The writing assignment is limited to producing one scene that is typical of the life of that hero.

Creative Thinking Skills to Be Developed: Looking from a Different Perspective; Being Original

Your students should get a slightly different view of the overused concept of heroism by responding to the items in the first part of the unit. They may have never thought of educator heroes or financial heroes. On the other hand, they are perhaps too familiar with the idea of athletic and entertainment heroes. In bygone days the great heroes were those who led nations and fought in wars. We may have fewer of those now than in previous times. In the United States, at least, a president is a hero to many and sometimes a bum to more, whether he or she leads the nation in war or not.

Preparing for and Presenting the Unit

Most authorities in the fields of psychology and child development believe that role models are important to young people. That notion has been looked at critically in recent years because the heroes have been reported to have feet of clay and minds of quicksand. We've always had journalists who loved to debunk heroes, pointing out flaws in their characters and myths about their lives, but in recent years the practice of examining the private lives of very prominent people has made it difficult for adults to find examples of exemplary men and women to hold up for their youngsters to emulate. Accordingly, by broadening the notion of heroism a little, we hope to encourage your students to see heroism in a light that differs considerably from the typical spotlight cast upon sports and entertainment figures.

You may find that your students just can't see heroism being demonstrated by financiers, writers, and educators. If that happens when they have taken a good look at the second part of the unit, you'll have an excellent opportunity to discuss the topic with them and to challenge the thinking of many of your students.

24 Heroism

5-Year-Old Saves His Little Brother

by the Associated Press

Puyallup, Wash.—A 5-year-old boy held his younger brother's head above icy water for 10 minutes before their mother could reach them in a frozen pond. Augustin Tudela, Jr., and his 3-year-old brother, Zacharias, were released Sunday from Madigan Army Medical Center after being treated for severe hypothermia.

"I don't want to sound overly dramatic," said the pediatrician who helped treat the boy, "but it's clear Augustin's intervention saved the 3-year-old's life. He was just tall enough to keep his toes on the bottom. He was able to keep his brother's chin and nose up. It easily could have been a tragedy where both kids were lost."

The boys' mother, Sandra Tudela, said she lost sight of them for only a moment while helping out at the Meridian Christian Ministries Church on Puyallup's South Hill. She thought they were chasing ducks near the shallow, frozen pond in front of the church.

"Then Augustin screamed real loud. Everything flew out of my hands and I started running and screaming," she said. "I tell you, I never knew I could run so fast in my life."

Tudela tried to run out on the ice, but she fell through. She waded in, pushing through with her hands as she gave Augustin instructions.

"I told my son, 'It's really important to listen to what Mommy has to say. You need to find your brother,'" she said. "He said, 'He's here! He's here, Mommy!'"

Tudela brought the boys to shore, where bystanders helped get them inside the church and rubbed them down until paramedics arrived. The boys on Sunday showed no visible effects of their ordeal. They romped in the living room of their Puyallup home as Tudela recalled the near-disaster.

Heroism *(continued)*

That is one kind of heroism, the kind we usually think about when we think of individuals as heroes. There are other kinds of heroes, of course, and the great majority of them never see their names in a newspaper. There is the heroism of a single mother who raises six children by holding down two jobs—and seeing every one of her children become professionals. You can undoubtedly think of many more.

Who will be the great heroes in the next few decades? Will they be athletes, singers, actors, comedians, politicians, evangelists, or city planners? Project yourself forward thirty years from now. What persons would be likely heroes in these fields? Describe them briefly, telling why they will be heroes.

law enforcement and jurisprudence

medicine

literature

public service

technology

finance

education

Now select the one individual among those heroes you have described who is most interesting to you.

Heroism *(continued)*

Write a scene that typifies that person's heroism. You can use the space below to outline the action and dialogue.

25
How Do You Say It?

An Invitation to Write Descriptive Paragraphs

Overview

Leading off the unit is a discussion of the importance of using fresh and forceful language. Your students are then asked to choose one of two adjectives to use in five sentences. The next level involves them in examining six clichés and offering alternative expressions for them. You are encouraged to substitute other clichés that are currently overly popular. Finally, your students are invited to write three paragraphs about the first home they will own or rent.

Creative Thinking Skill to Be Developed: Being Original

The message of this unit is to break free and try to avoid the trap of just going along with the crowd. So there is an attempt on our part to tell your students it is all right to be an individual and to express that individuality in their speech and in other ways.

Preparing for the Unit

This unit starts off with a lesson about synonyms and then proceeds to one about clichés, but throughout it is about the subject of variety in descriptive language. As we have attempted to do in "Like That" (unit 11) and "Feeling

Colorful" (unit 17), we would like to encourage your students to think of using language that is apt, powerful, and fresh rather than employing the same tired expressions.

The best time to present this unit is when you would like to call attention to the limited range of expression that restricts the ability of your students to speak and to write effectively. (Profanity and vulgarity tend to reduce effective speaking drastically, but those are not topics to be dealt with in this idea book.) "How Do You Say It?" can be used as a follow-up exercise to "Like That" (unit 11) because it tries to convey the same message about enlivening language by using fresh expressions rather than platitudes.

Presenting the Unit

At the first level, the student is asked to make choices between words in five pairs of adjectives that describe people's moods. The pairs of words in some of the sentences are very close in meaning, and in others they are further apart. We want your students to puzzle over their choices because choosing exactly the right word is very difficult for even professional writers, and anyone who writes is beset constantly by the problem. Being able to find just the right word is partially a matter of "feeling" what works and what doesn't in sentences and paragraphs. Since the sentences are not given in context, your students may properly complain that choosing the better word is impossible.

The second section offers six current clichés for the student to rewrite. They range from the unobtrusive "feeble attempt" to the hackneyed "Hang in there!" This is a formidable task for anyone because, for example, if brain damage is severe what else do we think of except "massive"? Similarly, what is an alternative expression for "Hang in there!"? The fascinating aspect of these two expressions is that twenty years ago one would rarely, if ever, hear "massive" used so indiscriminately, nor would one hear about "hanging in." Edwin Newman has a great deal to say (which clause, of course, is fairly trite in itself) about these and other expressions in his books. Perhaps your classes have used them in their study of usage and idiomatic expression.

The Writing Assignment

Our thesis is that students can write more effectively if they work at it. Writing three paragraphs describing the student's projected first home of his or her own is the challenge. For some, writing three paragraphs about anything constitutes a torturous assignment; for others, writing three paragraphs is no chore, but doing so without using a trite expression is nearly impossible. Neither type of student should be "let off the hook" (a platitudinous metaphor that proves to the authors how very difficult this assignment is). Insist upon three properly constructed paragraphs, and have your students go over and over their writing in search of tired expressions. As troublesome an assignment as this may be, it is doubtless a revealing one.

References

Edwin Newman's books about the deficiencies and pitfalls of American speech can provide you with a wealth of ideas for alerting young people to the drabness of their oral and written expression.

Newman, Edwin H. *Strictly Speaking.* Indianapolis: Bobbs-Merrill, 1974.

———. *A Civil Tongue.* Indianapolis: Bobbs-Merrill, 1976.

25 How Do You Say It?

1. There is considerable variety in the English language, but people generally use the same words and phrases to convey their thoughts, especially those people belonging to social groups. If the word or phrase is not accepted as a "regular, legitimate" part of the language, it is called slang. Despite the derogatory connotation, slang is used by nearly everyone, and most of us would be hard pressed to express ourselves if we couldn't use slang.

If we are to be more effective speakers and writers, though, we need to use expressions that are fresh, vivid, and forceful. Let's look at some "regular" English words and think of how effective they are in getting across an idea. First, let's look closely at descriptive words, or adjectives, as they might possibly be used in a short story. Choose one of each pair of adjectives in the following five sentences.

a. When Ned got up that morning, he was really *grouchy/irritable*. Which of the two adjectives is most effective in describing Ned's disposition?

Why is it more effective?

b. Marilyn found the key had been stolen from her desk drawer when she was called from the room, and the deception made her *furious/angry*. Which of the two words is more effective in conveying the idea of Marilyn's emotion?

Why do you think so?

How Do You Say It? *(continued)*

c. The big man's face was wet and *pink/florid* as he grunted and groaned under his great burden. Which word works best in this sentence to convey the color of the big man's face?

   Why do you think it is better?

d. After receiving the invitation, Jane's whole demeanor changed—instead of being depressed, she was quite *happy/elated.* Which word better describes Jane's behavior?

   Why is it better?

e. Raymond was sitting *rigidly/stiffly* in the booth, not saying a word, as the butterfly clung to his ear. Which of the two words works better in this sentence?

   Why do you think so?

   Which of the five pairs of words in the sentences above is most nearly synonymous?

   Which is the least synonymous?

How Do You Say It? *(continued)*

2. All words have shadings and connotations that often make it difficult to find exact synonyms when we speak or write. For example, *elated* and *ecstatic* are very much alike, but the degree of joy in *ecstatic* is greater than it is in *elated.*

Very often words come out together in groups. We call these groups of words phrases. As you know, phrases are used to convey ideas of all kinds. For example, we frequently hear of a "gracious host." That expression is used so often that we can consider it a cliché. Unless you are very unusual, you use clichés or trite expressions in your speech constantly. If you are interested in the number of clichés that you and your friends use, listen to a casual conversation today. You'll find that the same expressions are used over and over. There are other ways of saying "beautiful person" or "there's no way," but we rarely find ourselves using them. Can you think of different ways of saying these sentences?

a. *Hang in there!*

b. *Come on over—the more the merrier!*

c. *You're lookin' good.*

d. *She's busier than a one-armed paper hanger.*

e. *That was a feeble attempt.*

f. *There was massive damage to his brain.*

How Do You Say It? *(continued)*

3. Students can write with precision and power, but it takes a lot of energy. While your writing should be natural and unforced, it should also be vital and vivid. Why don't you see if you can manage to write in both ways?

Try writing a description of what you will say and do when you move into the first home of your own. Describe the way you think the home and its surroundings will look (and smell, too). Make your description at least three paragraphs long. You can use the space below for working out your ideas.

26
Nature

An Invitation to Write Haiku

Overview

Four kinds of poetry are featured in *What Next?*—namely, couplet, quintet, cinquain, and haiku. The first two are traditional verse forms, and the second two are miniature forms that appeal to young people in part because of their brevity. We are well aware that, from the second grade on, students in many places are asked to write haiku frequently. In the past forty years it has been one of the most successful devices for "turning on" children to poetry. We trust that by the time your students reach middle school and high school they may not have written haiku for a while, and the invitation to write a nature poem about the future will appeal to them.

Creative Thinking Skill to Be Developed: Being Original

Because haiku doesn't have rhyming lines, your students are more likely to write verse that is fresh and original than they might otherwise write when attempting to write poetry. The introduction of haiku into American schools has had a distinctly salutary effect upon the sensibilities of young people, who have learned to express themselves in a natural way.

Preparing for the Unit

Picking the right time to present the unit will be a matter of finding an occasion when your students are concerned about their environment. If a discussion does not evolve naturally from the students, you can introduce the topic with a news item about a crisis happening somewhere on the globe (for example, acid rain in Canada or a pestilence threatening to wipe out crops in California, Texas, Russia, Argentina, India, Ireland, or wherever.)

Presenting the Unit

At the first level, there is a brief discussion of nature, and a few examples are given about changes in Earth's terrain and weather. The student doesn't respond to any questions at this level, being "warmed up" only by the ideas presented.

There is a little more involvement at the second level, however, since the student is asked to think optimistically about forthcoming changes and predict a change that will be beneficial to the creatures of the Earth. If students are interested, some reading and discussing are in order. Scientists, futurists, and alarmists are continually predicting changes in the weather and the effects of technology, so there will be no dearth of articles for your students to read.

The Writing Assignment

It would be a good idea to have several examples of haiku available for your students, even though they are, in all probability, veterans of many a haiku writing session. If you don't have one or two handy, here is a classic haiku by the eighteenth-century poet Issa:

Hi! My little hut
is newly thatched I see . . .
Blue morning-glories.

One important reason for the popularity of haiku is that groups of young people take to it easily, and there is usually a high percentage of fresh, honest verse produced when it is assigned. Unless the timing is wrong, there is no reason to suppose your students will not compose very satisfactory haiku.

Closely related to Zen philosophy, haiku dates from the seventeenth century. It derived from the tanka, a five-line poem with a syllabic pattern of 5, 7, 6, 7, 7. The modern haiku is modeled after the poetry of Basho, who adopted only the first three lines, changing the last to five syllables.

The two elements of general scene and momentary impressions that characterize haiku stimulate the imagination and improve skills in word choice and usage inasmuch as the student learns to write it as he or she reads it. Haiku is quite different from the student's preconceived ideas of poetry, and it is refreshingly brief, thereby producing creativity with astonishing ease and rapidity. Since the poem will be grammatically correct, it is a simple matter to teach the rhythmic-melodic-lyric effect of unrhymed as well as rhymed poetry if you and your students have undertaken to produce poetry during the term.

Because of its disciplined form, haiku—either solemn or light, serious or frivolous, religious, satirical, or even humorous—will help students to overcome their negative attitudes toward poetry and correlate their reading and writing of poetry in a most creative manner. Artwork for a scroll or a poetry broadside can increase the attractiveness of the final products.

References

Behn, Harry. *Cricket Songs.* New York: Brace and World, 1964.

Henderson, Harold G. *An Introduction to Haiku.* New York: Doubleday, 1958.

Stewart, Harold. *A Net of Fireflies.* Tokyo: Charles E. Tuttle, 1960.

Ullyette, Jean M. *Guidelines for Creative Writing.* Dansville, N.Y.: F. A. Owen, 1963.

26 Nature

1. Many people believe nature is nature and, by definition, it doesn't change. For a great many years now, however, we have seen changes in the manifestations of nature. The terrain in many places has changed and is changing. Mountains have blown their tops and buried lakes, cliffs have slid into the sea, islands have appeared and disappeared, and rivers have changed their courses. Moreover, people all over the world claim the weather is changing. But is it getting colder or hotter? We hear reports of both. A great many species of animals and plants have disappeared from Earth, and more are feared to be on the way to extinction. Mother Nature may not be any different from the way she has always been, but there have been changes in the ecological conditions on Earth.

2. What changes in the natural environment do you predict for the next century?

   Write your list of the changes in the space below. Are any of your predictions of a positive or optimistic nature? __________ If not, think hard and come up with one or two ecological changes that will be for the betterment of the creatures living on earth. Which of these predictions is your favorite?

   Why is it your favorite prediction?

3. Here is a little nature poem—a haiku—about a fleeting perception of some manifestation of nature.

The cold atmosphere
Freezes the regular thoughts
Of an early Iris.

As you probably know, haiku is a Japanese verse form that has three lines of 5, 7, and 5 syllables. Sometimes, the poet may alter the syllables slightly. Haiku is very popular in countries other than Japan, though, partly because it gives a glimpse of nature that is usually lovely or charming. Why don't you think a bit more about the ecological change you envision for the twenty-first century and then write a haiku about it? It may take a few trials before your haiku comes out in an easy, "natural" way, so you will probably have to write two or three miniature verses before you produce one you are satisfied with.

To give you a better understanding of haiku, here is another verse and some information about its characteristics.*

A chilled lily floats
Below shifting horizons
Quavering at dawn.

Usually there is a visual image in the first two lines, and the third line jumps into a universal concept—the nature of the world. Frequently, a season is the backdrop, and the poem points up the interrelation of humans and nature. The subject is stated, and the location, time of day, or season is mentioned or suggested. Most important, the three lines must express or suggest thoughts, feelings, experiences, or observations vividly.

*This was composed by a tenth-grade student.

Nature *(continued)*

You can use the space below to write your haiku.

27
Joe Hunt's Image

An Invitation to Write a Bizarre Story

Overview

This unit is the traditional writing exercise inviting a student to "finish a story." The first four sentences set up the story line, and the student is to take it from there. Obviously, the exercise will be successful only if those first four sentences stir the imagination of the student. Since the theme of seeing in a mirror something different from the image of the viewer is not original with us, we'll make no claim concerning its power to inspire young people to write entertaining stories, but it is an example of the mystery/horror story genre that fascinates many people.

Creative Thinking Skill to Be Developed: Elaborating

A great many people are blessed with a wealth of novel ideas. The ideas come to them all of the time. Unfortunately, too many people who get novel—and oftentimes good—ideas don't follow through with them. They conceive of a melody, invention, recipe, story, design, or plan, but they don't develop their ideas. There are good reasons why some of these people don't follow through—coming up with ideas is a pleasurable activity for them, but developing their ideas is hard work.

Of course there are those very fortunate people who have a staff of assistants whose role it is to develop and bring to fruition the sparkling ideas of their creative leader. Very few of us are in that position, so encouraging young people to follow through with their ideas, wild and impractical though the ideas may be, is something you can do to help them gain genuine satisfaction in being fully functioning individuals.

Preparing for the Unit

Setting the stage for this unit should be relatively easy. The main factor is timing (as it usually is). You should administer the unit when your students are fed up with the everyday lessons of the curriculum. That, as we say, should be relatively easy, but you can pick a time when they have had a fairly steady diet of memorizing, recalling, and recognizing and few opportunities to express their own personalities.

Presenting the Unit

Whether the brief introduction at the beginning of the unit is read and discussed is up to you. There might be a reason for doing so because in that way you are endorsing the activity, and that is important. For some students an invitation to use their imaginations is a green light to get silly. Your students may be more mature, so all you need to do is to let them know you expect them to use their imaginations to produce a readable and interesting story. Each of them is capable of doing just that.

If you find it advisable to do so, having your students share their stories can be an entertaining and edifying follow-up. Look for common themes in their stories. They may be surprised that several stories are similar. If so, it would be a good idea for you and your students to try to determine why the stories have common themes. Such a procedure will help everyone understand the influences of television, movies, and novels upon young people, even when they aren't fully aware of these influences.

27 Joe Hunt's Image

1. Have you ever had the experience, a kind of premonition, of seeing things as they will be instead of the way they are now? Sometimes it is only a vague feeling. Sometimes it is the look of something; it isn't really the way it should be today—it is changed somehow.

2. Finish the following story about a man who sees himself as he would be three decades into the future. Take the story as far as you would like. In this instance, it might be well if you didn't make an outline first but just let the story carry you along.

Looking at himself in the mirror as he was shaving, Joe Hunt got a shock. Not yet 24, he was startled at the face that stared back at him, because it looked to be at least 55. And the gadget in his hand looked nothing at all like his razor. Yes, that face looked a lot like Joe, but there were differences—disturbing differences.

Joe Hunt's Image *(continued)*

Finish the story in the space below.

28
The Persevering Porcupine

An Invitation to Write a News Article

Overview

As the title indicates, this unit is concerned with alliteration. It starts with a news story that was written by a playful reporter and then proceeds to engage your students in a game that has them producing alliterative expressions for a variety of people and two inanimate objects. The unit culminates in an invitation to write a news story similar to the one about the persevering porcupine.

Creative Thinking Skill to Be Developed: Being Original

The creativity expressed by the reporter who wrote the news story isn't of a terribly high order, but it nonetheless wasn't the kind of writing commonly found in local newspapers. We don't expect especially original ideas to come from your students when they are exposed to these units. Our purpose is to nudge them in the direction of honest self-expression. Therefore, if your students produce a set of poor imitations of the persevering porcupine story, you shouldn't be disappointed. Like writers everywhere since the invention of writing, your students are learning by imitating other writers.

Preparing for the Unit

This exercise culminates in the writing of a news article, but the amount of journalistic training your students receive prior to writing the article is entirely up to you. There is no attempt in the exercise itself to point out the tenets of good journalistic writing, largely because the two purposes of the unit are to encourage the student to play around with alliteration and to think about the technological advances of the future.

Although the alliteration activities may seem unrelated to looking into "marvelous machines that haven't been invented yet," the creative process works best when the individual engages in a good deal of playfulness. Thus, we hope that in such a mood, your students will come up with a little ingenious thinking as well as some clever writing.

Presenting the Unit

The news item reproduced in this exercise actually did appear in a newspaper just as it is given. We feel it is an especially humorous piece.

Alliteration will always be with us, but it was especially in vogue during John F. Kennedy's presidency, when Ted Sorenson and Kennedy's other speech writers fell into an alliterative groove. Although alliteration can be overworked, students can use it from time to time with good effect. It is, after all, only one of many devices that can be used by a writer to gain the reader's attention. By no means is it as powerful in conveying images and meaning as is metaphor. Still, the catchiness of alliteration will appeal to a majority of your students, and this lesson could be successful on that basis.

The task set for the student at the second level—coming up with alliterations for eleven descriptions of workers and things—is fairly challenging. Perhaps students who play word games will fare better than those who don't play acrostics, anagrams, crossword puzzles, and the like. It should be emphasized that there can be more than one alliterative expression for any of the descriptions given. These are the ones that we had in mind when the exercise was devised, but your students might well come up with others just as good:

An automobile that is very full: crowded car, cramped car

A domicile that is supposed to have spooks: haunted house

A lawyer who makes a lot of mistakes: bumbling barrister, awful attorney

A very tight-fisted cleric: parsimonious parson, miserly minister, penny-pinching parson

An impish girl: mischievous maiden, mischievous miss

A spoiled child who is very intelligent: brainy brat

An officer of the law who is quite overweight: corpulent cop, portly patrolperson, portly police officer, fat fuzz, paunchy police officer

A corroded railroad track: rusted rail

A brave person who fixes pipes and valves: plucky plumber

A cowardly keyboard player: pusillanimous pianist

The Writing Assignment

Writing a news article with a multitude of alliterative expressions about an amazing new machine could very well be a challenging task for most of your students. With a little guidance from you, however, the assignment can be carried out fairly easily. First of all, the student must have some "marvelous machine" to write about, so a little research is in order. We have stipulated that the machine has yet to be invented, but perusing scientific, futuristic, and other kinds of periodicals can easily provide the inspiration for the idea of a new machine. Machine is a word that is applied to all manner of contraptions, gadgets, contrivances, vehicles, and mechanisms, so the range of possibilities is very wide.

Second, with so much alliteration packed into the article, the intent is to amuse as much as it is to inform the reader. Therefore, you can advise the student to have fun when he or she sits down to write the article. Local newspapers often run tongue-in-cheek pieces such as the one in this exercise. It's something that larger regional newspapers like to do occasionally, too. A piece such as this is a relief from the gloomy and unsettling news articles that seem to predominate these days.

References

If your students need some help in getting ideas about future machines, you might refer them to one of the following references or a similar one:

Panati, C. *Breakthroughs.* Boston: Houghton Mifflin, 1980.

Rose, S. *Future Facts.* New York: Simon & Schuster, 1976.

28 The Persevering Porcupine

1. This item appeared in a newspaper and amused many of its readers.

Perambulating Porcupine Prickly Perseveres

A porcupine that panicked a private party Tuesday posed perplexed police a prickly problem.

But Patrolman Ken Behrend, proceeding with poise and protocol, provided a peaceful solution.

Behrend answered a call at 10:30 P.M. at the home of Lawrence B. Grisson, 973 Hilyard St., where the porcupine had walked uninvited up the front steps and down into a basement.

After despairing of taking the porcupine prisoner, Behrend reluctantly pounded it with his patrol stick—powerfully.

Then he ported the departed porcupine to the dump in a paper carton. When he got there, lo, he found the porcupine very much alive.

So he gently released it to its native habitat and it scampered off into the woods.

Practically prancing.

The literary device that the reporter so lavishly employed in this piece is called alliteration. When successive words, or words near one another, have the same initial sound, the speaker or writer is using alliteration. It is all around us—in the names of businesses (Kut and Kurl Room, Kopper Kitchen), in the titles of songs ("Sweet Sue," "The Sounds of Silence"), in the titles of books and plays (*Zen and the Art of Motorcycle Maintenance, Secrets of Successful Fishing, Games People Play, The Man of La Mancha*), in the names of products (Tonka Toys, Perma Press), and in the nicknames of teams (Purple People Eaters, Bronx Bombers).

2. Let's find out how good you are at coming up with alliterative expressions. Produce an alliterative phrase for each of these:

An automobile that is very full

A domicile that is supposed to have spooks

A lawyer who makes a lot of mistakes

A very tight-fisted cleric

An impish girl

A spoiled child who is very intelligent

An officer of the law who is quite overweight

A corroded track

A brave person who fixes pipes and valves

A cowardly keyboard player

The Persevering Porcupine *(continued)*

3. You can test your alliteration skill by writing a news article similar to the one about the porcupine. Instead of writing about an animal, write about some marvelous machine that hasn't been invented yet.

   Imagine you are a reporter for a newspaper ten years from now and your editor has given you an assignment to write about this amazing new machine. You can sketch out your ideas for the article in the space below.

29 What's Going On?

Invitation to Imagine a Solitary Sensing Time in the Future

Overview

The unit should constitute a change of pace in the day-to-day school experiences of your students (always a welcome happening). If you can manage to do so, allow your students to pick a spot on the school grounds for their observing. They should do so individually and noiselessly. In the experience of many teachers, this activity of having students sit quietly and record what their senses are receiving works quite well, but it does require the cooperation of all your students. Once situated in places of their own choosing, they are to monitor what is going on without moving or speaking.

After returning to the classroom, your students are to select one or two of the experiences they have just had and write about them. Their thoughts can then be put into the form of a jingle, limerick, song, or poem. Then your students are asked to do some thinking about how successful poets, painters, sculptors, composers, and architects get their ideas. Finally, they are to imagine what this activity would be like in the future.

Creative Thinking Skills to Be Developed: Being Sensitive and Aware; Being Original

The two creative thinking skills to be developed in this activity are alike in an important way—they are fundamental and essential to creative production.

Being open to what is taking place inside and outside the individual is a prerequisite for thinking creatively. Without this openness the individual soon becomes restricted and imitative in her or his thinking.

As for being original, without that element in the individual's thinking, the resultant behavior cannot be "creative." The product of the thinking does not have to be novel in a world-changing way, but it must be novel in the individual's intellectual history to be labeled "creative."

Preparing for the Unit

In one sense, the time to introduce this activity is any time. Before we can think productively we must be alert to what is going on around us. Our perceptions are the raw material out of which ideas, hunches, and theories are formed. However, some time of the day or the week may prove to be more suitable than others for this more-or-less sedentary activity. For some classes it might follow a more active segment of the curriculum, such as physical education, with good results. On the other hand, many classes conceivably might not be able to sit quietly after the excitement a physical education period often produces. Try it out when you think your students can profit most from an exercise of this kind.

Presenting the Unit

After they have completed the awareness activity, your students are to turn in their papers to you. Their impressions should prove quite interesting, if not enlightening, and some of their observations may surprise you. Thus, you will have a chance to see how your students differ in their perceptions. We recommend that you return their papers, unmarked, on the following day. When your students look at their papers a second time, they themselves may be surprised at their observations.

Although all writers must be sensitive to their surroundings, poets especially rely upon their senses. They seem to be able to see things that the rest of us never notice, even when we find ourselves in identical situations. In a word, poets are more "alive" than the great majority of other people. The purpose of "What's Going On?" is to make your students more aware of what is taking place in their own immediate worlds—to help them become more alive.

If the awareness activity is successful in causing your students to marvel at what they can learn when they use their senses fully, some of them will want to put their impressions in poetic form—if they are given an opportunity to do so. Undoubtedly, some of your students will not be eager to write a poem, but you can make the assignment more palatable to those who are reluctant to write verse by allowing them to treat any subject they wish and to choose any form of poetic expression that is congenial to their ideas and to their personalities. If you have not discussed the essential qualities of poetry with your class, this will provide you with an opportunity to get across some fundamental points about what makes poetry the delightful genre it is. Unrhymed verse often will not qualify as poetry, but it can be the beginning of more successful attempts in this idiom. And, of course, if someone writes lines that rhyme, she or he is not necessarily writing poetry. An excellent way to deal with this dilemma is to have your students compose haiku or cinquains.

Your students should be assured that their ideas are the principal consideration and that they should strive to put their feelings in a form that is meaningful to others who have had similar experiences. However, since they are not actually required to write a poem at the second stage of the unit, your students should not feel in any way coerced into producing a poem.

The final section concerning the differences a student's grandchild might have participating in the same activity nudges students' thinking in a direction that causes another kind of reflection, namely, that the phenomena of the world are transient. Everything changes.

Following through with the Unit

The results of this unit may or may not be apparent in your students' behavior after it has been administered to them the first time, but if you repeat the activity (with your own variations), you should notice that their perceptions are keener and that they are aware of phenomena that they had not noticed before. It might be a good idea to have them compare their earlier papers with subsequent ones to see if your students do become progressively more alert. Accordingly, if your students have folders or notebooks in which they can file this unit, ask them to keep their observations. Many teachers find that in asking their students to collect their writings they are demonstrating that these productions are worthwhile. Since it is extremely difficult to persist in doing something as demanding as writing without receiving some form of encouragement, showing your students that their efforts have value is absolutely necessary in a successful language arts program.

This encouragement, however, does not require that the teacher correct and grade everything turned in. If poems are to be published in a school magazine or in some other way, your students will want to proofread what they have written. Young people like to hear the poems that other young people have written, and they like to hear their own poems read aloud. Above all, young people should not be afraid to trust their teachers with their first struggling attempts at verse making. If you correct and mutilate everything they write, fear will inhibit their writing. Furthermore, if you are too bent on correcting or appraising the poems your students write, you are likely to be unable to grasp what they are trying to convey on deeper levels and to maintain touch with the unconscious operations of their minds.

29 What's Going On?

1. Follow the directions for this activity stated below:

   a. Find a comfortable spot in the room (or, if possible, outside the building) and sit quietly for ten minutes. Try to be aware of what is going on around you and also what is going on inside you. Are there things around you that you have never noticed before?
   b. Do not share your observations with others.
   c. Write down what you see, what you hear, what you smell, and what you feel.
   d. When you feel that you have described accurately all that you are aware of, turn in this paper to your teacher.

What's Going On? *(continued)*

2. Now that your teacher has returned your paper and you have had a chance to review the different sorts of impressions you had yesterday, some of your observations may prove particularly interesting to you. Take one or two of the most promising ideas and do some thinking about them. Then write these ideas on this piece of paper. If your ideas show some relationship to one another, you might like to make some notes about how they relate. If only one idea appeals to you, elaborate on it by jotting down other ideas that come to you when you think about it. When you have done a good deal of thinking about your ideas, put your notes in some form that can eventually be made into verse.

Your Interesting Impressions

Developing Your Ideas

What's Going On? *(continued)*

Organizing Your Ideas

Here is some work space for you to use in developing your poem, jingle, limerick, or song.

What's Going On? *(continued)*

3. How do you suppose great poets or composers get their ideas? Do you think that all of their ideas are good, or do you suppose they discard or change many of their ideas?

   Write your suppositions in the space below.

4. Imagine it is a time in the future and you have a grandchild. If your grandchild were told to go to a spot and record for ten minutes all of the impressions his or her senses give him or her, would his or her experience differ from yours?

   See if you can think of at least five differences that might exist between the experiences you and your grandchild could have had.

30
Garbled Grammar

An Invitation to Write a Limerick

Overview

By putting together the pieces of nine sentences that have been jumbled, your students will probably have composed one or two odd statements. The activity is supposed to get them in the mood to write limericks, and the chances are fairly good that will happen unless they take the piecing together too seriously. Task-oriented students occasionally find no mirth but some grief in doing the warm-up activity of "Garbled Grammar." Assure that type of student that it isn't important to put together the nine sentences exactly as the authors wrote them.

Creative Thinking Skill to Be Developed: Being Original

Limericks are supposed to be somewhat nonsensical, and therein lies their charm. Their appeal is in their humor. Unfortunately for would-be limerick humorists, some limericks are merely bizarre or foolish. Admittedly, we have been guilty of writing strange limericks occasionally. Some people think that with practice limerick writers can improve. You can test that hypothesis with your students.

Preparing for the Unit

The activity that leads off the unit is the familiar one of putting the pieces of a puzzle together. In this case the pieces are nine sentences that have been torn into three parts each and randomly scattered into three columns. The task is to assemble the parts into nine sentences again.

An attitude of playfulness in engaging in this activity, as is true in most games, is the critical factor for its success. If he or she has a "creative set," the student will enjoy the activity and come up with a few surprising or amusing sentences. Therefore, the mood of your students should not be too terribly sober when this unit is administered. It would not be a good idea to present it when your students are anxious about an exam.

Presenting the Unit

So there won't be any temptation on your part to regard some of your students' sentences as "correct" or "incorrect," we won't give you the original nine sentences. The sentences don't really have to be the original ones; they just have to be sentences, even if the directions ask the student to "put them together as they were written originally." The idea is to discover unusual or zany combinations. It is quite important that you make this point because there are students who get frustrated with tasks such as this one. It takes a little patience to get the nine sentences together.

The Writing Assignment

In contrast to most of the other units of *What Next?* the second-level activity has the student composing. Since the point of mixing up the sentence fragments is to have the student put together a humorous sentence or two, the limerick, an essentially humorous form of verse, was chosen as the type of writing the student would engage in.

The limerick offered as an example in the unit may or may not be sufficient to give your students an example of the genre. You probably will want to give other examples by Edward Lear and other writers who have excelled at writing limericks. Here is one of Lear's famous limericks:

There was a young lady of Wilts,
Who walked up to Scotland on stilts;
When they said it is shocking
To show so much stocking,
She answered, "Then what about kilts?"

The final activity of the unit involves the student in speculating as to the possibility that one or more of the zany sentences that were concocted may turn out to be true. For instance, "Bankers with generous instincts are soon unemployed" has a certain amount of plausibility. Many of your students' sentences will make perfectly good sense, of course, but the "crazy" ones are the ones that they should examine for their credibility.

30 Garbled Grammar

1. The following groups of words were originally nine separate sentences. They were fairly reasonable statements about classifications of people. Each sentence was broken up into three parts, and then all of the parts were mixed up as you see them below. Let's find out if you can put them together as they were written originally.

stifle a yawn
who love their work
Gentlemen
Morons
to come up with new figures
Clowns
whose favorite topic is "me"
don't get the picture
who have a lot of charm
to improve their minds
Con artists
need lots of help
are soon unemployed
can make a good living
People
have few inhibitions
Bankers
with generous instincts
ladies
must throw off old ways
who lose their composure
Dieters
who gossip in hallways
are sometimes left in the cold
Photographers
who don't want to offend
need to broaden themselves

Garbled Grammar *(continued)*

Write the sentences as you think they were originally written.

2. Do you think any of the zany sentences you concocted will turn out to be nearly accurate? For example, you might have come up with a sentence such as "Dieters who lose their composure are sometimes left in the cold." Is it just possible that dieters could do something that would leave them out in the cold if they lost their poise? Which sentences might stand as fairly good predictions?

   Explain why those conditions might be likely ones.

Garbled Grammar *(continued)*

Did some of your sentences turn out to be a little crazy? Which two or three were the oddest or funniest?

3. Since combining these fragments into sentences often leads to some peculiar notions, you might want to take one and turn it into a limerick. The traditional limerick is a humorous piece of rhyme that has five lines and a definite rhythmic pattern. The first, second, and fifth lines rhyme, as do the third and fourth lines. Very often a limerick starts with "There was a . . ." You don't have to begin your verse that way, though. Here is an example of a limerick that has the rhyming scheme and the rhythm that are necessary.

Whenever I witness a yawn,
Whether produced at midnight or dawn,
I strain to refrain
From airing my brain
Until the affliction is gone.

If possible, the last line should have a twist or some element of surprise.

Think about one of your zany sentences, and then jot down some ideas that spring from it. You will find it a challenge to keep to the rhyme scheme, but the more you think about your sentence the more rhymes will pop into your head.

31
Scientific Liars

An Invitation to Write an Anecdote

Overview

This unit begins with a rather long introductory discussion of the matter of telling the truth. We could say "the tricky business of telling the truth," but that would be distorting the issue somewhat. The great majority of people want to tell the truth most of the time, and we don't view making statements as being characteristically "tricky." The point we make is that what is absolutely true is often hard to ascertain.

There are three parts to the unit. In the first part we try to make a case for the notion that people lie when they don't mean to and tell the truth sometimes by accident. It is perfectly all right if one or more of your students disagree with us—in fact, we hope someone does. At the end of the discussion, the student is to consider eight statements and label each true or false.

The second part of the unit gives the student an opportunity to comment about occasions when truth and falsity are deliberately mixed together. The third section is an invitation to write about some happening in the future.

Creative Thinking Skill to Be Developed: Being Original

In a way, this unit is a straightforward creative writing activity. It leads up to an invitation to your students to write an anecdote that takes place in the future. Before they get to that point, however, they are to play around with the somewhat puzzling—and occasionally slippery—notion of telling the truth. In our culture the topic is an important one; it would be just about impossible for a young person to have escaped hearing about truthfulness many times prior to encountering this unit.

If we have been successful, your students will be truly original when they write the short piece about the future. They will have tussled with the eight statements in the first section and tried to think of instances when the truth was deliberately mixed with lies in an intent to delude. These experiences should incline your students to thinking independently, and that should result in writing that is comparatively free of the influence of prescribed patterns.

The discussion about truth relates to the writing activity because people who write about the future are indeed interested in being as accurate as they can be. Accordingly, we are trying to persuade your students to write plausible pieces, not wildly bizarre or ridiculous nonsense, about future events.

Preparing for the Unit

We can imagine a number of topics that could lead in nicely to "Scientific Liars," ranging from plagiarism to political speeches. Truthfulness has become an increasingly important issue in national affairs, and it will probably continue to be a very hot issue. If we are correct in this prediction, you will have many opportunities to lead in to the unit with events of the day.

Presenting the Unit

Your sharper students will probably point out a flaw in the introductory section of this unit, namely, that one does not really lie unless one is deliberately saying something known by oneself to be false. The intent of the speaker or writer is the crucial matter in lying. For the sake of our argument, we don't deal with this point. We are not trying to say that truth is relative to the situation in which a statement is made. We are trying to say that people can't always be so certain that a statement is absolutely true or false.

The unit culminates in an invitation to the student to write a short piece of fiction. We offer several possible topics, but only because there are students who prefer to have a topic suggested and dislike having to think up one for themselves. The little list of topics we provide may or may not be appropriate for your class. You may want to add a few items that seem more provocative.

"Scientific Liars" might best be extended over two class periods because the discussion generated in the first and second sections may take a while. Moreover, it might be a fine idea to allow some time to elapse before your students undertake the writing activity. They can benefit from talking it over with others and deliberating the ideas on their own.

31 Scientific Liars

1. Occasionally—perhaps more often than we think—a person lies and doesn't know it. A statement can be made in all sincerity, and the individual will be telling an "untruth." There are also many times when a person has intended to tell a lie but, instead, as it turned out, was telling the truth. So it behooves us to think twice before calling anyone a liar. People who intend to tell the truth often don't and those who intentionally lie occasionally tell the truth. What do fiction and fact have to do with science? Everything. The history of science is actually the history of miscalculations, misinterpretations, and falsehoods. Nevertheless, scientists, more than most people, want to tell the truth.

Let's examine some statements with regard to their truthfulness. Label each of these statements "false" or "true," writing out either word to the left of the statement.

_______ Blondes have more fun.
_______ It is impossible to paint well if your feet are freezing.
_______ Children from broken homes are likely to run up large credit card balances after they marry.
_______ People from Georgia are called "Georgia Peaches," not "Crackers."
_______ Computers are a source of pleasure, confusion, and pain.

______ Because they are used to driving on snow and ice, midwesterners purchase fewer traction devices for their tires, on average, than people in the Pacific Northwest.

______ Hunting animals is a cruel and juvenile activity.

______ Dentists are individuals who like to work with their hands and are insensitive to the pain of their patients.

2. Some of the statements above are opinions—they are true for some people and not for others. Others contain an element of falsehood mixed in with what seems like truth. In true-false examinations, a statement is false if any part of it is false. Maybe life isn't like that. Maybe a lot of things contain elements of both truth and falsity.

Sometimes deceit, chicanery, and fraud are packaged right in with veracity, integrity, and honesty. Can you think of an example?

3. Verifying statements is what scholars and reporters do. Writers of fiction don't have the bother of worrying whether everything in a story is absolutely true or not, but they must have settings that are historically accurate or at least seem to be correct for the time and place of the story.

What about writers of science fiction? Do they worry about the truthfulness or accuracy of what their characters say and do? Yes, they do, but because they write about events in the future, they have more leeway in guessing correctly or incorrectly.

Why don't you try your hand at predicting the future, as science-fiction writers do? You can choose from any of the topics below, or any other of your choice. Write an anecdote—about two pages—concerning an event that might take place twenty years from now.

Scientific Liars *(continued)*

An incident at a secondary school
An accident involving two vehicles
An incident where a theft occurs
The party after a marriage ceremony
A scene after an athletic event
A musical event witnessed by two people in their mid-forties

32
Opposites

An Invitation to Write a Dramatic Skit

Overview

After a brief discussion of synonyms and antonyms, the unit involves your students in producing antonyms for a dozen words having some relationship with the future. The unit culminates in an invitation to write a drama based upon conflict. The conflict is to be suggested by one of the dozen sets of antonyms students came up with in the activity. You may want to expand the list or have your students supply their own conflicts.

Creative Thinking Skills to Be Developed: Seeing Relationships; Being Original

Conflict, tension, and dichotomy are three themes revered by teachers of literature. We didn't go into the theme of conflict very deeply in this unit, but we hope the unit involves your students enough in the idea of opposing forces that they will see some interesting relationships and attempt a play based upon their perceptions.

Preparing for and Presenting the Unit

By the time students have reached high school, lessons in synonyms and antonyms are behind them, but anyone who writes is continually searching for synonyms and antonyms. As students, the members of your class are required to write, and thus the beginning section of this unit may be of some benefit to them.

If presented earlier in the year, "Opposites" can be used to reintroduce your students to the thesaurus, which is really a treasure trove for a writer. The list of words for which they are to find antonyms—all dealing with the future in some way—is a challenge if a dictionary or thesaurus is not used. As far as learning is concerned, it would be best if your students tried to come up with good antonyms without referring to anyone or anything. After they have mentally dug a little, they can profit more from the thesaurus or dictionary.

The words chosen for this vocabulary exercise are all associated in one way or another with the time dimension. Many of the words, such as *infinite, prediction, endure,* and *forever,* pertain to the future. As noted earlier in this book, our intention is to persuade the student to think about the future. We try to do this by coming at him or her from different directions. Finding antonyms for the first two words, *yesterday* and *late,* will pose no problem for any student whose native tongue is English, but from that point on antonyms may be harder to come by. What *is* the opposite of *space?* Nonspace? What's that? Certainly there are students who can expound about what nonspace is, and we hope you have one or two in your classes. Similarly, if *now* is synonymous with the *present,* is its antonym *then,* the *past,* or the *future?* Incidentally, are *forever* and *infinite* really synonymous?

The Writing Assignment

The discussion and thinking that make up the first two parts of the unit are to prepare the student to write a short play or dramatic skit about the future. Our assumption is that students, in thinking about one or more words for which they have produced antonyms, will think in terms of conflicting people and events and thus be started on the way to a scenario for a short play or dramatic skit. The instructions encourage students to think of collision-type conflicts for which they see no logical, rational solutions. The idea is that as they become creatively involved with their characters and their conflicts, they will think of imaginative and surprising solutions that they could never have produced through logical reasoning.

As with the other units in *What Next?* we have provided space for working out the first ideas for the conflict, the characters (protagonists), the setting, the situation, and the like. We leave it to you to decide how much instruction is needed regarding the elements of dramatic writing. If you or your students need a resource, we suggest *The Art of Dramatic Writing* by Lajos Egri (1960). The chapter on conflict is especially valuable and so are those on character, scenes, and dialogue.

Reference

Egri, Lajos. *The Art of Dramatic Writing.* New York: Simon Schuster, 1960. (Available in paperback)

32 Opposites

1. There are many words in our language for which we can substitute other words that are approximately the same in meaning. Words that can be interchanged without altering the essential meaning of a sentence are called synonyms. Familiar examples of synonyms are verbs such as help and aid and adjectives such as fast and swift.

Similarly, there are words that have opposite, or nearly opposite, meanings. These words are called antonyms. Easily recognized pairs of antonyms are *happy* versus *sad*, *full* versus *empty*, and *deep* versus *shallow*.

Not every word of English, however, has a synonym or an antonym. Adjectives, nouns, and adverbs are more likely to have antonyms than are nouns, prepositions, and conjunctions.

2. See if you can find a word that means the opposite, or close to the opposite, of each word on the list below. Don't use a dictionary or a thesaurus unless you are really stuck. If you can think of more than one good antonym, underline the one you think is furthest in meaning from the word that is listed.

What is the opposite of

yesterday?

late?

space (n.)?

repeat?

Opposites *(continued)*

(the) past?

nuclear?

now?

(to) endure?

forever?

(a) prediction?

(to) judge?

infinite?

3. You may not have had to resort to using a dictionary or a thesaurus when you produced antonyms for the dozen words listed here. On the other hand, you may have found it very difficult to come up with a word that is really the opposite of one or two of the words that we listed.

For which single word did you have the most trouble finding an antonym?

Opposites *(continued)*

Is that the one that interests you most? If so, why don't you do some thinking about the ideas involved in that word and its opposite(s) or some other word on the list that especially interests you? Your ideas will probably cause you to think in terms of people and events and the conflict that results from their opposing values, motives, or characteristics. This should give you the basis for a drama, play, or skit. Characters for your drama or skit should come readily to mind when you think about the word and its opposite(s) and so should the setting. The action should take place some time in the future and should have at least two main characters (or protagonists).

Using separate sheets of paper, you can name your characters and outline the conflict. Try to think of a conflict for which you see no logical, rational solution. As you involve yourself with your characters, you will doubtless be able to think of a solution that will surprise you.

Write your drama in the space below. Be sure to give your drama or skit an intriguing title. The nature of the conflict or your surprise solution may give you an idea for such a title.

33
Punny Names

An Invitation to Name Unborn Offspring

Overview

The first part of the unit is a punning game. It leads to more punning and then to an invitation to your students to name their unborn offspring. For a good many young women and men, thinking of names for their future children is a familiar pastime. There are fashions in names, of course, and if your students engage in this part of the unit several years before actually becoming parents it is likely they will change their minds about some of their choices when they actually become parents.

Creative Thinking Skill to Be Developed: Combining Ideas and Elements

The first game involves your students in matching first names with surnames, and the second part does the same thing. Therefore, we have an activity here that all parents engage in when they choose first names for their babies—one of the simplest applications of the skill of combining ideas and elements. The idea of the games is to find names that will be appropriate for the surnames. In so doing, puns of a rudimentary sort are produced rather naturally.

Preparing for the Unit

This is a change-of-pace unit. It can be administered at any time, although since it involves your students in playing with words, it might precede curricular activities such as writing humorous pieces and reading fiction featuring picturesque names for characters. (Hawthorne and Dickens are just two of many authors who have used punny names.)

Presenting the Unit

As is the case with all of these units, there are really no correct answers to our questions. In most cases some responses are more appropriate, clever, or original than others, but if an off-the-wall answer works, so be it. Because we did have names in mind for the ten items in the first section, we'll list them. They are not to be considered the only suitable responses, however.

- *Art* Hunter
- *Philip* Carr
- *Hi* Singer
- *Ray* Fisher
- *Bunny* Hopper
- *Heather* Gardner
- *Sue* Laws
- *Robin* Fowler
- *Page* Turner

There are quite a few Art Hunters and Ray Fishers around, but perhaps not so many Page Turners.

The second section might be a little challenging for some of your students. They might have to think hard for an appropriate nickname for a Parsons or a Kidd. Beach ("Sandy"), Forrest ("Woody"), and Barber ("Butch") should be relatively easy.

The last section has your students thinking up names for their progeny. If they claim they won't be having any, you can just allow them to skip that part of the unit—or perhaps suggest they think up names for a friend.

33 Punny Names

(Er, What Shall We Call Her?)

1. Originally, many people derived their names from their occupations. A Taylor sewed clothes. A Smith worked with metals such as iron, gold, and silver. People rarely work at jobs their forebears had when the names were first bestowed, but it would be convenient if they did. For example, if Mr. and Mrs. Beyer could predict their daughter will have a job as a purchaser of flowers from nurseries for a florist, they might name her Rose or Iris. She would then be called Rose Beyer or Iris Beyer, of course.

A number of other appropriate first names could be given to babies if only their parents could predict that their children's occupations would follow along the lines of their surnames. Let's suppose that these people might try to predict their son's or daughter's future calling. What names would these people give to their babies?

- Mr. and Mrs. Hunter have a son and foresee that he will purchase paintings for a gallery. He will probably be called __________, the diminutive for _________.
- Mr. and Mrs. Carr expect that their son will be working in the automobile service business, probably in a gasoline station. They might call him __________.
- Mr. and Mrs. Singer might foresee that their son will naturally use his voice, perhaps becoming an opera singer—a tenor. They will probably name him __________ so that his nickname can be __________.
- Mr. and Mrs. Fisher predict that their son will go underwater to spear mantas. He'll be known as __________, the diminutive for __________.

Punny Names *(continued)*

- Mr. and Mrs. Hopper foresee their daughter as a dancer who will specialize in novelties involving groups of people. They'll call her _________.
- Mr. and Mrs. Gardner anticipate that their daughter will be a landscape architect specializing in ornamental shrubs imported from the British Isles. They will name her _________.
- Mr. and Mrs. Laws have a baby daughter and foresee she will live up to her name and be an attorney specializing in cases involving injuries. Her first name might be_________, and the diminutive would be, appropriately enough, _________.
- Mr. and Mrs. Fowler see their girl capturing songbirds and banding them. They might call her _________.
- If Mr. and Mrs. Turner had the foreknowledge that their son would someday assist concert pianists on the stage, they could call him _________.

2. People with last names such as Rhodes and Rivers often are tagged with nicknames such as "Dusty" and "Muddy." What would be good nicknames for these surnames?

_________ Barber

_________ Forrest

_________ Kidd

_________ Links

_________ Parsons

_________ Beach

Punny Names *(continued)*

3. If you have children, you probably won't bother to give them punny names, even if your surname is Cook and someone suggests that your son be called "Bernie." But let's say you will become a parent one day and you are faced with the task of naming your offspring. You might as well do some thinking about it now.

Guess how many children you'll have, their sexes, and give them names. Write your list in the space below. You might keep the list because it could come in handy (and it might amuse you later on).

34
Thirty Is All You Get

An Invitation to Write a Television Commercial

Overview

"Thirty Is All You Get" starts with a discussion of television commercials, a form of entertainment your students know as well as any other. After a few questions about commercials, your students are asked to assume the role of a writer and produce a thirty-second "spot."

Creative Thinking Skill to Be Developed: Being Original

Since writing TV commercials is a demanding job that takes a good deal of experience and talent to do well, we wouldn't expect extraordinary scripts from your students resulting from their encounter with this unit. Quite the contrary, we would be amazed if they produce anything that actually could be used on the local community service channel. But stranger things have happened.

It might be expedient and productive to have them work in groups of three to five. As a matter of fact, these productions are undertaken in that way—"group think" is the norm. Popular entertainment is usually the product of the synergistic creativity of people in groups.

Preparing for the Unit

A discussion of television or television commercials, which are so much an integral part of the medium, would lead in perfectly to the administering of this unit. It is called, rather obviously, "Thirty Is All You Get" because the task is to write a thirty-second commercial. As network rates go, if the commercial is to be aired in prime time, the cost of such a project would be enormous. But you may want to mention that fact only in passing. There is no need to put the pressure on the writer, as the agency and producer would do in real life. Scriptwriting is different from other types of writing, and so before presenting the unit or administering the writing exercise itself, you should discuss script-writing as a special form of the storytelling art. We provide a format of a script at the end of the unit, but you might want to give your students another format to follow. The exact format is not a matter of great importance, but there must be general directions concerning camera movement, audio background, lighting, and setting. If there is narration, it is handled a little differently from straight dialogue.

Presenting the Unit

The point of the unit, however, is not to provide training for aspiring television writers. Our intention is to entice students into just writing. We felt that a short writing task that has the attractions of being a different kind of assignment and the likelihood of offering the student a little fun would make writing seem like something else. Since nearly every young person is exposed to television and probably talks about the commercials, the decision to include a unit that calls for television writing seemed plausible.

After an introductory section about the television of the future, your students are to select a product, a setting, an activity, and some characters, cafeteria style, from the four lists of elements of a commercial. High school students should have no trouble following the instructions for making the choices, but one or two of your students may want to circumvent the rules. That would be quite all right—as long as a script is produced. The smorgasbord process is only a way of involving your students in the scripting, as well as a device for their coming up with some bizarre or zany situations to script.

The Writing Assignment

There might be some straight scripts produced by your students, and there might be a lot of offbeat scripts written, too. If your students follow the directions to the letter, there should be more offbeat scripts than honest attempts at writing a good television commercial. If the writing is imaginative and fresh, you won't care if it is the kind of script that a writer would seriously offer to an agency or not.

On the other hand, the format (or one like it) should be followed, and the tenor of the entire production shouldn't be too hokey. The students should attempt to be skillful in handling the usual considerations of plot development and climax, even though this is a different form from regular story writing.

The medium is television, but people are always surprised to find out that sound is terribly important. "The script is everything," some producers say, and we say that the words spoken are usually the most important element of the script. That can be forgotten easily by directors and cameramen who get carried away by the visual elements of the filming. Because of time limitations, your students will realize that a few words have to do the job. A verbose scripter of television commercials is by definition an unemployed one.

Reference

Millerson, Gerald. *Effective TV Production.* New York: Hastings House, 1976.

34 Thirty Is All You Get

1. Since you probably have seen thousands upon thousands of television commercials, you rate as an expert about them. In some ways filmed television commercials have not changed very much in the past dozen years, but in other ways today's commercials are different from those made just a few years ago.

   In your expert opinion, how have commercials changed since the time before you started to go to school?

   Do you think television commercials will change much more in the next twelve years? If so, in what ways will the filmed commercials (as opposed to the live commercials from local stations) change?

Thirty Is All You Get *(continued)*

Did you mention new products? If not, what new products might be advertised on television in the years ahead?

2. Imagine that it is twelve years from now and you are a scriptwriter working for an advertising agency that has landed a contract to do a thirty-second commercial for a nationally advertised product. You can write a script in any way you like, but you must choose as your product either one of the new products you have listed or one from the first column of the following chart. And you must also use only one of the settings and actions in the following chart, but you can use as many of the characters in the third column as you wish. For example, if you just chose the first items of the four columns, you would have a commercial selling a beauty aid featuring a clown at a race track involved in a small riot, and you could also bring in other characters such as the psychoanalyst and the movie actress.

There is a sample television script at the end of the unit to illustrate a format you can use. However, you do not have to include all of the technical instructions. You should include the instructions for the action that will accompany the dialogue, as well as filming instructions.

Thirty Is All You Get *(continued)*

Remember: you can have only thirty seconds of edited film for your commercial.

Product	**Setting**	**Characters**	**Actions**
beauty aid	race track	clown	small riot
household cleaner	space station	homemaker	wedding
automobile	laundromat	musician	birthday party
beer	supermarket	movie actress	political rally
finance company	beach	lion tamer	breakfast
deodorant	pig farm	computer programmer	space shuttle
dentures	city street	sanitary engineer	therapy session
weight reducing salon	big outdoor amphitheater	tour director	under-way commute
aspirin	underwater tunnel	marathon runner	rock concert
hair dye	dump or landfill	psychoanalyst	shopping

After you have made your choices, write them down in the spaces below.

Product (give it a name):

Setting:

Characters:

Action:

Thirty Is All You Get *(continued)*

You can use the space below for jotting down ideas about how you'll sell the product.

Thirty Is All Your Get *(continued)*

Sample Television Script

(Visual directions are on the left, and audio directions are on the right. Sound effects are underlined. Three cameras are used in this scene.)

Title: Suddenly
Scene: 3
Location: Kitchen
Time of Day: Afternoon

SHOT CAMERA
FLOOR POSITION
20 2 D

CU PAT's hands, showing him counting coins. PULL SLOWLY BACK to CU, stopping at door knock.

21 1 B

CU Door latch ZOOM OUT to MS as door opens.

22 3 C

MCS of MIKE sprawled on floor.

23 2 D

2s HOLD PAT as he comes round table.

24 1 B

CU Back of MIKE's head. We see he is injured. He looks up at Pat.

TILT UP to MCU PAT.
(Pat is seated at table, a box before him, from which he takes gold coins. There is a knock at the door.)
SFX Knocking on door

PAT: What do you want?

PAT: Who's there, I say!
SFX Thumping on door

(Door latch rises. A body falls in, onto floor.)

PAT: What in the name of . .

MIKE: It's me. I've got to see you.

PAT: What's wrong with you, man? Are you drunk or something?

PAT: Don't lie there. Get up and tell me what you want.

35
The Poor Boy Who Was Rich

An Invitation to Write a Short Story

Overview

This unit starts with a discussion of given names, proceeds with a guessing game about the origins of ten well-known names, and ends with an invitation to write about the interaction of three people twenty years hence. Your students are induced to do a good deal of thinking about the reasons why people give their children certain names. Then they are asked to reverse the familiar business of giving fictional characters names that are appropriate and to write a very short story in which they give three characters names that are ironically inimical to the characters' personalities and circumstances.

Creative Thinking Skill to Be Developed: Being Original

As is often the case in these units, your students are asked to do some convergent thinking before they are invited to think divergently. It's a loose form of convergent thinking, though. "The Poor Boy Who Was Rich" challenges them to guess the original meanings of names such as Vincent and Carolyn before asking them to write from two to four paragraphs about an incident twenty years away.

Preparing for the Unit

An obvious time to introduce and administer this unit is nearly any occasion when a name in a story is especially suitable for the personality the author has given the character. Charles Dickens gave some of his characters remarkably colorful and appropriate names, but he was by no means the only great writer to do so. Picturesque names abound in literature.

Presenting the Unit

The names children are given have changed considerably in the last generation. It may be, then, that the ten names we've asked your students to look up are not common ones in your school. Where Deborah once reigned (often as Debbie) along with Jennifer (not so often as Jenny), other names for girls have replaced them. On the other hand, there would be nothing wrong with your students looking up Estelle, Vincent, Marvin, and the rest. The names we have chosen aren't completely out of style yet. Another plan would be for you to substitute the common names of young people in your school for the ones we have provided.

The writing activity of the unit logically evolves from the warm-up, but it requires a good deal from your students, who must invent three characters and transport those characters in time to an incident that shows that they all have been perversely named. On the one hand, that assignment represents quite a bit of thinking; on the other hand, the little plot will reveal itself fairly easily once the characters and their names have been decided upon.

35 The Poor Boy Who Was Rich

1. Have you ever known anyone whose name belied his or her personality or circumstances? For example, have you known a poor person named Rich? Have you ever known a boy named Frank who was devious or a flake named Ernest? It's interesting to learn what a given name originally meant; for instance, Harold is an old Germanic name meaning "leader of the army." Robert meant "bright with fame" originally. Nadezhda, the Russian for Nadine, means "hope."

What does your name mean? ______________________________
If you don't know, most larger dictionaries will tell you.

2. Guess what these names originally meant. Then look up the names and write the correct meanings to the right of your guesses. (They can be found in larger dictionaries.)

Name	What You Guess It Means	Real Meaning
Marvin	________________	________________
Estelle	________________	________________
Deborah	________________	________________
Vincent	________________	________________
Andre	________________	________________
Phyllis	________________	________________
Patricia	________________	________________
Reginald	________________	________________
Carolyn	________________	________________
Frederick	________________	________________

The Poor Boy Who Was Rich *(continued)*

3. Since names are important to people (there is evidence that some people tend to try to live up to their names), writers of fiction have often amused themselves by giving their characters fitting and colorful names.

You might practice being a writer of fiction by writing from two to four paragraphs about an incident twenty years from now that involves three people. The three people all have been misnamed, and the incident brings out the irony of their names. Choose names for your characters that are in great contrast to their personalities and circumstances.

36
What Drives You Crazy?

An Invitation to Write an Editorial

Overview

This unit has to do with everyday annoyances and pet peeves. After considering a number of common annoyances, your students are asked to write an editorial about something that rubs them the wrong way.

Creative Thinking Skills to Be Developed: Elaborating; Being Original

This unit requires your students to build an argument in the form of an editorial. That task calls for the skill of elaborating upon a main idea. Students will have to look for facts, find examples, and expand ideas in order to build a case for their points of view. Although editorial writers may not think of themselves as skilled elaborators, they most certainly are.

Preparing for the Unit

This unit has annoyance as its theme, and so you can expect some reactions when your students encounter it. In the same way that "Windless Sails" (unit 19) is designed to provoke some rather strong feelings, "What Drives You Crazy?" is meant to get the pencils moving because your students, like the rest of us, are subject to daily vexations and annoyances.

Although an appropriate lead-in is always important in setting the stage for presenting a creative writing activity, your approach to this unit will probably be brief and unrelated to the foibles of your students. A literary tie-in might work best. If your students are reading stories (including news stories) that feature frustrating habits or idiosyncrasies, you can introduce this unit by citing an example of that kind of behavior.

Presenting the Unit

After an introduction about petty annoyances, the student is invited to imagine that he or she has the resources to avoid any annoying bit of behavior on the part of people he or she encounters daily. The student is able to prevent the annoyance from happening, so she or he is able to imagine actions for blocking, avoiding, negating, or otherwise escaping the verbal behaviors and the motoring behaviors of the nine annoying types. There is a mixture, then, of fantasy and realism in the unit.

The Writing Assignment

The real world is the subject of the writing activity as the student is invited to write an editorial about one of the situations with which he or she has just dealt hypothetically. If none of the situations in the unit is provocative enough, the student can name another annoying habit that he or she would like to see eradicated. A few words about the nature of an editorial are offered, and then we ask the student to come up with three main points and have supporting statements for each.

It may very well be that some of your students have journalistic experience. If so, you may want to have them discuss with you and the class the characteristics of a good editorial. Having the journalism students share their knowledge and views is a better pedagogical ploy than merely lecturing about the theory of editorializing.

36 What Drives You Crazy?

1. Most of us have our gripes about the petty annoyances of everyday living. Unless you are unusually easygoing and tolerant there are a number of things people do that incur your ire. These experiences often change our mood and spoil the day for us.

In most cases there isn't much we can do about the irritating behavior of the offending person. But let's fantasize a bit. Suppose you had all the resources in the world you might need to prevent these disturbing events from happening to you. What would you do to avoid them?

Here are a few common annoyances. Think of how you might deal with them if you had any resource at your disposal. What would you do about

a. People who cut in front of you in line?

Or people who invite others not in line to join them in front of you?

b. People who repeat everything they say ("It really gets me, you know, it really gets me")?

Or people who can't seem to repeat anything they have said that you missed? (It annoys them to say anything twice.)

What Drives You Crazy? *(continued)*

c. People who don't finish their sentences?

Or people who finish sentences for others?

d. People who look at everyone else while talking with you?

Or people who stare at something you are wearing the entire time you are talking to them?

e. People who hang up just as you get to the telephone?

Or people who always let the phone ring four times?

f. Motorists who always drive in the inside lane no matter what their speed or the speed of the traffic?

Could we eliminate this problem by means of technology in the future? If so, how?

g. What about motorists who roar up close behind you (tailgate) no matter whether you can change lanes or not?

Would an advance in technology eliminate this problem or not? Why or why not?

What Drives You Crazy? *(continued)*

h. Motorists behind you who honk as soon as the traffic light changes?

In the years to come, how do you think this problem can be solved?

i. What about motorists ahead of you who never seem to notice that the light has changed until it is impossible for you to cross the intersection in time?

How can we eliminate this problem in the future?

2. Why don't you write an editorial about one of the gripes above, or another one that annoys you even more? An editorial is a persuasive commentary, written by an editor, about a current situation. It is often, in effect, a little thesis intended for the readers of a periodical and written from a particular point of view. As such, this thesis is an argument and thus needs facts to support it, so make sure you have verifiable statements to support the position you take in your editorial. Maybe you have never been the editor of a newspaper or magazine before. This will give you a chance to get something off your chest. You can sketch out your main points and supporting statements in the space below.

Your thesis (argument), briefly stated:
Main point 1:

What Drives You Crazy? *(continued)*

Supporting statements:

Main point 2:

Supporting statements

What Drives You Crazy? *(continued)*

Main point 3:

Supporting statements:

Your rough draft of the editorial can be based on the material you have written in the previous exercise. Write it and your finished editorial on separate sheets of paper.

37
Traps

An Invitation to Write an Essay

Overview

The unit leads off with a pseudo classified ad and then leads your students through a series of questions about traps. It ends with an invitation to write an essay about a trap.

Creative Thinking Skill to Be Developed: Looking from a Different Perspective

The simplest example of the ability to see things from a different perspective is the hackneyed question posed about the half-empty/half-full glass of water. It can also be dramatically demonstrated by the perceptual trick of presenting the old hag in the drawing of the girl, or vice versa. As an everyday practical matter, however, seeing things differently from one moment to the next is most inconvenient. If you can see both sides of a question equally, you may be a good arbiter but a lousy decision-maker.

On the other hand, creative people do see things differently. It occasionally gets them in trouble, but more often it gives them satisfaction and even joy. This unit is designed to get your students to look at life a little differently—and to give them a bit of satisfaction in doing so.

Preparing for the Unit

In this unit the students are asked to play with the concept of "traps" and then to write an essay about a trap. Any time of year is a good time for administering this unit, but it could be presented when your students are trapping game or shellfish (if those pastimes are popular in your area). It may also appeal to those of your students who are more reflective. There is very little humor inherent in this unit, although your students could bring forth a little humor or irony in their responses.

Presenting the Unit

The classified advertisement that initiates the unit is similar to none your students will ever see in a newspaper, as is declared in the opening sentence. It isn't meant to represent a legitimate classified ad, of course; its purpose is to seize the reader's attention briefly as he or she tries to determine what the exercise is all about. The exercise is all about traps, although the question following the ad queries the student about time's importance to him or her.

At the second level, the student is asked to think of traps for six abstractions, starting with fame and ending with fidelity. Then the student is asked, "Which of the above items would you most like to capture or have captured for you?" Finally, the student is asked what *else* he or she would enjoy trapping. Open-ended questions such as these are more likely to be revealing than convergent-thinking questions, and they also provide opportunities for the student to get away from thinking of situations as right or wrong. Because students can respond to a unit such as this one in a personal manner, you may want to leave the responses on their papers and not discuss them with the entire group unless there seems to be a need to share ideas. On the other hand, if there are clear indications that the class would enjoy and benefit from a discussion of some of the ideas brought out by the unit, an enlightening discussion might better prepare your students for writing their essays.

The Writing Assignment

Essays aren't terribly exciting writing assignments for some young people. The word has stodgy, pedantic connotations. Therefore, you may want to suggest the possibility that the essay about traps could be done with tongue in cheek—both serious and humorous essays would be acceptable.

If your students are well acquainted with the essentials of an essay, you will only have to refresh their minds about the essay's characteristics. "Sweet Success" (unit 12) culminates in an essay and has four points about the essay listed at the end of the unit. If one unit precedes the other by not too great a period of time, it should be an easy matter to reinforce the learning that took place in the previous assignment.

37 Traps

1. You probably will never see an ad such as this in the classified section of your newspaper.

> **WANTED**
> One time trap! To be employed in halting the swift passage of this precious dimension; to allow exploration of the often ignored wonders of our planet and of human achievement; at a pace that would enrich rather than superficially absorb.

Of all the tangible and intangible things you might trap, would you choose time? Why or why not?

2. Although time may or may not be the most precious thing you could trap, there are other intangibles that would be worth trapping. Can you think of some natural (or unnatural) traps for the following?

fame

sorrow

wisdom

enthusiasm

humility

fidelity

Which of the above would you most like to capture or have captured for you? __________ Why?

What else would you very much enjoy trapping? __________ Why?

3. Why don't you write an essay about some kind of trap? Select a situation or process that particularly intrigues you, amuses you, or disturbs you.

A good essay is both interesting and persuasive. That is, the essayist marshals ideas in such a way as to inform and influence the reader. Organization is very important. Arrange your ideas in a logical manner, placing the strongest points in the beginning and closing sections of the essay. Use examples to give the reader a clear understanding of the points you are making and also to enliven the essay.

Traps *(continued)*

You can jot down your reflections in the space below. Then organize your ideas into some kind of outline before you write your rough draft on separate sheets of paper.

38
FREE!

An Invitation to Write a Scenario or Science Fiction Story

Overview

A discussion of the overused word *free* leads off the unit, and then a number of questions are posed regarding the matter of how free a variety of things really are. These questions lead to an invitation to write a futuristic story dealing with someone who was mistaken about something's being free.

Creative Thinking Skills to Be Developed: Looking from a Different Perspective; Being Original

As Torrance (Torrance and Safter 1990) states, "Being able to see things in different visual or psychological perspectives has been the essential ingredient in nearly all inventions and innovations" (93). In this unit, the perspective that is slightly unusual is that we often deceive ourselves. We know of the deception, but we ignore it. The authors' intention, however, is not to encourage your students to be cynical, but just to be more perceptive.

Preparing for the Unit

This unit deals with one of the most overworked words in the English language. It is also one of the words with the greatest amount of emotional loading. Thus, it should be examined by your students—and they probably have done so in class before—because of its importance. Cynics claim that there is nothing that is truly free in the world. The truth of that contention depends, of course, upon the definition of free one gives. No definition is given in the unit, but by the time the student has reached the writing activity he or she will have come up with more than one good working definition of the word.

You can use this unit in conjunction with many curricular activities that involve students in thinking about what is gratis or about the concept of freedom, or you can simply introduce it with a comment or two about something that is being offered free. (There is always a time when something is being offered "free.")

Presenting the Unit

This unit has three steps leading up to the writing activity. At first there is a discussion of the ways in which merchants and politicians use the word. Both groups use the word as a come-on, but the merchant uses "free" as an opportunity to "get something for nothing" and the politician uses "freedom" as a *right* of the individual or a group of people.

The second part of the unit involves the student in making judgments about the "free-ness" of such things as birthday presents and sidewalks. The last item, affection, was included so as to bring out the idea of the mutuality of a friendship—something is expected in return, although people will deny it.

At the third level, the student is asked to think about what things that are free now will not be free in the years to come. This is perhaps as profound a question as any in this book. You may want to spend some time in discussing the possibilities of losing what we consider to be our freedom, especially if your students have been reading *Brave New World, 1984,* or *Walden II.*

The Writing Assignment

After reflecting at length about whether freedom implies the incurring of an obligation, the student is asked to write a scenario or futuristic story about someone who mistakenly believes something to be free. There are two kinds of deception implicit in the mistaken notion that something is free: another person misleads the protagonist or the protagonist misleads himself or herself.

We deceive ourselves all of the time, of course, and sometimes we do it rather consciously. We know, for example, that the extra brush attached to the box of detergent isn't really free—we have to pay for it. Nevertheless, it appeals to our something-for-nothing acquisitiveness. Similarly, we believe that if we obey the rules we have the freedom to drive our cars on the streets, but the streets are not cost-free. Most of the time we'd just prefer not to think about the tax money it takes to build and maintain streets.

References

If you want to encourage students to write scenarios, you may find very helpful the handbook on scenario writing prepared for use in the national Future Problem Solving Program. It has chapters on the characteristics of scenarios and their major functions, specific instructional techniques, the evaluation of scenarios and talking with students about their scenarios.

Torrance, E. P., B. Blume, J. Maryanopolis, F. Murphey, and J. C. Rogers. *Teaching Scenario Writing.* Cedar Rapids, Iowa: Future Problem Solving Program, Coe College, 1980. (Price: $2.50)

If you want to encourage students to write science fiction stories, you will find very useful Ben Bova's *Notes to a Science Fiction Writer.* In fact, the suggestions given by Ben Bova in this book are useful in teaching any type of story writing, and the book includes excellent suggestions and practice exercises on character development, the creation and handling of conflict, plot development, and the like.

Bova, Ben. *Notes to a Science Fiction Writer.* 2d ed. Boston: Houghton Mifflin, 1981.

Torrance, E. Paul, and H. Tammy Safter. *The Incubation Model of Teaching.* Buffalo: Bearly Limited, 1990.

38 FREE!

1. The word free is used a lot in advertising and politics. There isn't a day that goes by that something isn't offered "free" in the newspapers or through the mails by a merchant or supplier. This kind of free often implies a giveaway or bonus. The word is very popular with politicians, demagogues, and "freedom fighters." In the context of the human rights movement, it has definite connotations.

What are the connotations of "free" in the context of the human rights movement?

We often hear expressions such as "free as a bird." What does that mean?

We also hear about air being free, and sometimes water, depending upon where the water is found. But we rarely hear about free land. Why do you think that is?

FREE! *(continued)*

2. So, whereas there are times when "free" means something extra to be given when you enter a door, purchase an article, or send in a coupon, it means something quite different in the sphere of human rights, where it is a fundamental and not an extra. Are the following things free?

A birthday gift from a friend? __________ Why or why not?

Wildflowers? __________ Why or why not?

A balloon at the opening of a market? __________ Explain.

The city's sidewalks?__________ Explain why you think so.

The beach? __________ Why or why not?

Affection from a girlfriend or boyfriend? __________ Why or why not?

3. Are there things that are free now that won't be free in the next century?

List some things that are free now that won't be free in the next century.

Explain why they won't be free.

4. Why don't you write a futuristic story about someone who thought he or she was getting something free and found that he or she was mistaken? The person can be misled deliberately, or there can be a realization that what was thought to be free really wasn't. See if you can expand upon one of the ideas you listed in section 3 and develop it into a scenario or a science fiction story.

Write your futuristic story in the space below, using additional pages as necessary.

39
Rhyme's the Thing

An Invitation to Write a Limerick

Overview

The three parts of "Rhyme's the Thing" are comprised of a warm-up in which your students translate two or three words into two words that rhyme; another little game like the warm-up, featuring rhymes that might play a part in their future; and an invitation to write a limerick. The rhyming activities are designed to set the stage for the limerick writing, and we anticipate that your students will have little trouble writing one.

Preparing for the Unit

This unit might be considered one that is fun for most young people. It shouldn't require much preparation on your part. Rhyming fits into several places in the language arts curriculum, but this particular unit probably shouldn't be used in conjunction with the teaching of poetry. Limericks are verses, of course, but authorities don't consider them to be poetry. In their opinion, rhyme doesn't necessarily equate with poetry.

Presenting the Unit

It's probably best for your students to tackle the first two parts of the unit individually. They can compare answers after finishing the second section. The warm-up activity should not be especially challenging for your students. Nevertheless, as with a crossword puzzle, anyone can get hung up on an item. For the purposes of this unit, it isn't important that your students spend much time puzzling over the little word games. Our intention is just to get them in the mood for limerick writing.

Here are the rhymes we had in mind:

- exactly correct—quite right
- corpulent dog—round hound
- pig's clothes—hog's togs
- yellowish-brown adult male—tan man
- genuine azure—true blue
- ugly woman's boast—hag's brag
- very warm scenario—hot plot
- a town's compassions—city's pities
- cybernetic vehicle—computer scooter
- extraterrestrial competition—space race
- sufficient goods—enough stuff
- lots of occupations—gobs of jobs
- scarce ursine mammal—rare bear
- time for wages—pay day

It is possible your students will come up with other answers.

The Writing Assignment

Limericks are easy to write—that's part of their appeal—but sometimes it is necessary to rewrite them several times. That was actually the case with the example given in the unit. Because of the trite moon-tune-June-spoon rhyme we used for illustration, the theme came all too readily to mind. But the rhythm of a limerick requires a certain number of syllables per line, and it took a full hour to compose the limerick. Your students will probably be much quicker and better at this than we were. It should be borne in mind, however, that, although an easy form to follow, the limerick can be a source of frustration.

39 Rhyme's the Thing

1. The limerick is a beloved, and often maligned, form of light verse. It is not poetry, nor does a writer of limericks pretend to be a poet when he or she writes five lines of mirth. The two principal ingredients of the limerick are rhyme and humor. A limerick that doesn't make some claim to humor, however slight, is not really a limerick.

Probably the reason there are so many limericks being written is that people enjoy writing them. Maybe the fun in writing a limerick is greater than the fun in reading or hearing one. The enjoyment arises partially because limericks are easy to write.

Let's prove the truth of that last statement. To get you in the mood to write a limerick, play this simple game. Translate the words in the left column that follows into two words that rhyme. To illustrate, if we give you the phrase "ancient ore," you could respond "old gold."

exactly correct ______________________

corpulent dog ______________________

pig's clothes ______________________

yellowish-brown adult male ______________________

genuine azure ______________________

Rhyme's the Thing *(continued)*

ugly woman's boast ________________________________

very warm scenario ________________________________

a town's compassions ________________________________

2. Now try the following pairs, which are things that might be in your world during the next twenty years.

cybernetic vehicle ________________________________

extraterrestrial competition ________________________________

sufficient goods ________________________________

lots of occupations ________________________________

scarce ursine mammal ________________________________

time for wages ________________________________

3. Select one of those six rhymes and add some more rhymes to them. The rhyming should get you in the mood to write a limerick. As you know, a limerick has five lines. The first two lines and the fifth line rhyme, and the third and fourth lines rhyme. If possible, the fifth line should have an element of surprise. For example, if you chose a rhyme such as moon swoon, you might think of these rhyming words: boon, tune, soon, goon, Muldoon, and June. You might then come up with a limerick along these lines:

A lad by the name of Muldoon
Serenaded a lass named June.
"I would feel like dancing,
Or even romancing,
But I can't stand that goon," said June.

Rhyme's the Thing *(continued)*

If you find you can dash a limerick off rather easily, try for a second and even a third.

40
Bumper Ads

An Invitation to Compose Bumper Sticker Messages

Overview

This unit is comprised of an introductory paragraph about bumper stickers, an activity in which the student is to match bumper stickers with the descriptions of five drivers, and another activity that requires the student to compose bumper stickers that might be on cars twenty years from now.

Creative Thinking Skills to Be Developed: Combining Ideas and Elements; Being Original

The two creative thinking skills to be developed in this unit are combining ideas and elements and being original, but the emphasis in "Bumper Ads" is on your students' using their imaginations to think what the world will be like in twenty years. They will have to project themselves into the future in order to guess what the crusades, issues, vanities, humor, and fashions will be like after two decades. It's likely, of course, that their stickers will be highly influenced by today's bumper stickers. Encourage them to stretch their imaginations and come up with highly original messages.

Preparing for and Presenting the Unit

Since this unit doesn't require as much time to complete as do many of the others in *What Next?* you can introduce it as a change of pace during a class and have your class compare bumper stickers at the next session.

Even though there isn't a lot of writing to be done, your students should do a good deal of thinking. They should have some ideas about the directions in which our society is heading sociologically, politically, and economically. Having some information about trends in those areas will make the unit easier and more satisfying for them. Otherwise, their bumper sticker messages will be mute echoes of today's sloganeering.

40 Bumper Ads

1. Quite often when a car passes, you see it has a bumper sticker. Some stickers are whimsical; some are polemical. You might see "I ♥ Tennis" on one bumper and "Arms are for hugging" on another. More and more bumper stickers have political messages. On bumper stickers all over the country, humor is illustrated and personal preferences and politics are proclaimed. Frequently you can get a good idea of what the owner of a car is like by reading his or her bumper sticker. Occasionally, you can be surprised because the message and the driver don't seem to go together.

What kinds of bumper stickers might the following people have? Either invent a message or match the person with a bumper sticker you have seen.

- Male, about 35; long, dark hair; long beard; dirty jacket; 10-year-old pickup truck with a dirty windshield.

- Female, about 19; medium-length blonde hair; pretty; stylish sweater; late model sports car with no dings on it.

- Male, about 55; balding; clean shaven; bespectacled; blue business suit; shiny luxury sedan with custom license plates.

Bumper Ads *(continued)*

- Male, about 22; short blond hair; good looking, muscular; t-shirt; moderately priced two-door sedan with two dings on the driver's side.

- Female, about 50; gray-brown hair styled for convenience; average looks; bespectacled; somewhat overweight; recent model compact car that hasn't been washed lately.

- Female, about 30; black hair; dark complexion; white dress with long earrings and red scarf; heavy luxury car recently purchased (dealer's name where plates would be).

2. Although bumper stickers can be considered a relatively recent fad in our society, they have now been seen for a great many years. It seems likely that they will be seen for a great many more. But will the messages be the same? What will bumper stickers twenty years from now be proclaiming? Try to think of what catchy sayings, slogans, complaints, warnings, promotions, and so on, will be seen on the bumpers of cars two decades from now. Invent a bumper sticker for each of the following categories:

Political slogan

Clever saying

Warning

Bumper Ads *(continued)*

Promotion

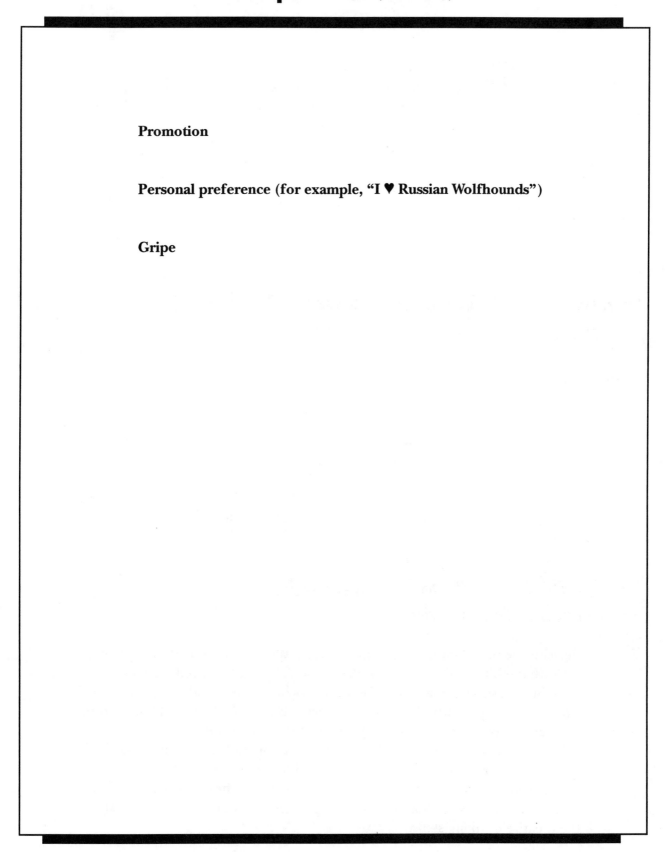

Personal preference (for example, "I ♥ Russian Wolfhounds")

Gripe

41
The Compulsive Buyer

An Invitation to Write a Character Sketch

Overview

This unit is in two parts. The first part presents your students with the dilemma of inheriting a lot of odds and ends from an eccentric maiden aunt. (Judging by the list of items she left, the aunt was a live wire.) The decisions your students make will be exactly the kinds they may be called upon to make later in life. The second part of the unit has them reflecting upon eccentric people or "characters" they have known and then writing a character sketch about one person who has caught their fancy.

Creative Thinking Skills to Be Developed: Being Flexible; Being Original

Perhaps the most famous of all of J. P. Guilford's original tests for measuring creative thinking abilities was his "Brick Uses Test." It consisted only of the examinee's listing as many uses for a brick as he or she could think of. If the examinee thought entirely of ways in which a brick could be used for building, no points were given for thinking flexibly. But if the examinee could also see a brick as a weapon, door stop, hammer, decoration, and so on, a high score for flexibility was awarded. Similarly, if your students can think of some other uses for the candle snuffers, bowls of artificial fruit, cat leashes, and so on, they are demonstrating flexibility in their thinking, often one of the most practical of the creative thinking skills.

If your students happen to know some very interesting persons, the writing activity could be enjoyable and relatively absorbing. Writing an accurate depiction of someone that is also entertaining and coherent is hardly easy, however. Organization is one key and description is another in making a personality sketch work.

Preparing for the Unit

"The Compulsive Buyer," like any of the other units in this book, is better suited to some groups of students than to others. It is not expected that all of the activities suggested will work for any particular group. On the contrary, we would be very surprised if your class were enthusiastic about all of the units. Inasmuch as one of the desired outcomes of each of the units is to have your students engage in some form of creative writing, there is a sameness in the content of these materials, and for this reason, "The Compulsive Buyer" may provide some relief from the emphasis upon words that is present in most of the units. If your group is not the kind that enjoys problems of the sort presented in this unit, you might hold it for an opportune occasion when the subject of eccentricity, inheritance tax, cats, or compulsive buying is brought up. Once again, you will be the best judge of when to introduce the unit—or whether it should be administered at all.

Presenting the Unit

The warming-up activity of "The Compulsive Buyer" involves the student in a situation that has confounded a great many people. If you have ever been bequeathed an old and nearly worthless piano or a box of rusty fishing gear, you know how difficult a position such as the one posed in this unit can be. Accordingly, the unit requires the student to do some practical thinking about how he or she might benefit from this peculiar inheritance. The student will have many factors to take into consideration as he or she thinks about what use can be made of these new possessions. How can they be used, if at all? How much would it cost to repair the objects or to make them complete? Will the student want to try to sell some of the objects? Which ones should be discarded or given to a charity? If some have to be discarded, will the student have to pay to have them hauled away?

Although this exercise is not meant to be a lesson in economics or in junk dealing, practical problems of the sort sketched out in "The Compulsive

Buyer" are likely to release the imaginations of many students who are disinterested in exercises that are remote from their everyday lives. Be on the alert for students who find uses that are not obvious; they may be young people who have undiscovered talents.

Following through with the Unit

If your students are enthusiastic about the idea of writing about colorful people they have known, it could well be that some very interesting sketches will result. Those writings that have special merit might be accepted for publication in the school newspaper or school magazine. Others can be read aloud or displayed on a bulletin board. You will have a chance to point out the elements (phrasing, diction, organization, and so on) that contribute to the success of a short piece of this kind when you discuss the sketches with the group and with your individual students. If you have a class discussion about the sketches, ask your students to generalize about what makes a personality sketch interesting. Much of what your students offer should be of genuine benefit to them in subsequent writing assignments.

You will be surprised at how complete and adequate the list will be. You may be interested, however, in comparing the list that your students compile with the following list of characteristics used frequently in assessing the interest level of a piece of writing:

- Conversational tone
- Naturalness
- Use of quotations
- Variety in kind of sentence
- Variety in length of sentence and structure
- Personal touch
- Humor
- Questions and answers
- Feelings of characters

In making this comparison, you will want to question the extent to which these general criteria can be applied to personality sketches.

41 The Compulsive Buyer

1. Suppose that your maiden aunt died a few months ago and when her will was read last week you were informed that she had left everything to you. However, in this case "everything," unfortunately, does not mean money. It means fourteen cats and a houseful of assorted objects. She had always rented her house (including its furnishings and appliances), and so you are required to go over to where she lived and remove your new belongings. You know that your aunt was a compulsive buyer and that she continually bought things she didn't need, and so you are both curious and apprehensive about what you will find. When you get to the house, this is what you find:

1 spray gun (without paints)
32 pounds of pottery clay
19 cases of cat food
1 set of cassettes for learning to speak Arabic
6 bowls of artificial fruit (purchased at a department store sale)
1 dulcimer (bought at a music store's clearance sale)
27 player piano rolls (but no player piano)
1 loom (with a broken shuttle)
1 innerspring mattress (spare)
1 small kiln for firing pottery
8 cat leashes (extras)
1 exercise bicycle
1 pearl-handled magnifying glass (for reading)
1 stereopticon (with 73 pictures)
1 beach umbrella (broken)
1 18-inch marble bust of Chester A. Arthur
5 pewter candelabras
6 brass candle snuffers
1 pair of water wings

The Compulsive Buyer *(continued)*

What can you do with all of these objects, which are now your possessions? Will you be able to use all of them? Will you have to throw some away? Which ones will you give away? Outline your plans in the space below.

The Compulsive Buyer *(continued)*

2. Do you know any eccentric people? When all is said and done, although they may frustrate or bewilder us, eccentric people add a great deal of color and excitement to our lives.

Of all the people you have known, who is your favorite "character"? Why don't you write a sketch of this person in the space below, pointing out why he or she is unusual and lovable?

42
A Vile Violinist?

An Invitation to Use Alliteration in a Paragraph

Overview

The three parts of this unit are (1) a discussion of syllabic alliteration, ending with questions about whether four alliterative descriptions of occupational workers are examples of syllabic alliteration; (2) a challenge to come up with syllabic alliterations for ten occupational workers; and (3) an invitation to use two or more of those alliterative expressions in a paragraph about a community the student may live in twenty years hence.

Creative Thinking Skill to Be Developed: Being Original

There are two kinds of originality that are called for in the writing activities of this unit. The first is composing syllabic alliterations for the ten occupations, and the second is incorporating two of the alliterations in a single paragraph. Of the two tasks, the latter is probably a bigger challenge. Turning out alliterative phrases is of a lower level of original thinking. Using alliterative expressions meaningfully requires some planning and organizing. This arranging, organizing, and editing is the essence of thoughtful writing.

Preparing for the Unit

We are confronted by a good deal of alliteration every day of our lives—in newspapers and magazines, on television and radio, and on billboards, posters, and flyers. Therefore, you can cite any one of the many examples of alliteration with which your students are familiar. They should be able to remember a few offhand when you introduce the topic, and they can find a great many more without undue effort. If, by chance, there is an example of alliteration in a curriculum material, you will have a good opportunity to point out how often the device is used.

Presenting the Unit

You won't find many, if any, discussions of syllabic alliteration in textbooks. As a special kind of alliteration, it occurs often enough, but it isn't especially valued by writers or critics. Nevertheless, to write syllabic alliteration poses more of a challenge for the writer than does general alliteration. In addition, as an academic exercise, distinguishing syllabic alliteration from the general kind will make your students use their ears inasmuch as they will have to make distinctions between sounds.

Once again, the writing exercise at the end of the unit requires that the student look into the future and try to imagine what the world will be like. This time, it is his or her own community. What will it be like in twenty years? Some understanding of developing trends in government, labor-industry relations, and demographics will be helpful in undertaking the writing of the paragraph.

42 A Vile Violinist?

1. You are probably quite familiar with alliterations, a common device in writing and speaking. Occasionally a speaker or writer goes beyond the repetition of initial sounds in a phrase or a sentence and repeats the initial *syllables* of words next to or near one another. For example, if you said something about a "powerful police officer," you would be using simple alliteration, but if you were to talk about "Polish police" that would be an alliteration of syllables. Similarly, a "carping carpenter" would be another example of syllabic alliteration, but puny pundit would not be (although punny pundit would).

What about "demented detective"? __________ "garish garage mechanic"? __________ "liberal librarian"? __________ "vile violinist"? __________ Are they examples of syllabic alliteration?

Use a dictionary to see if you are correct.

2. See if you can make up syllabic alliterations for these occupations.

maid____

salesclerk____

mayor____

printer____

sailor____

seamstress____

engineer____

barber____

typist____

welder____

A Vile Violinist? *(continued)*

3. Now put two or more of your alliterations in a paragraph describing the people of your community twenty years from now.

Write your alliterative paragraph in the space below.

43
Business

An Invitation to Write a Vignette

Overview

This unit is simply an exercise in writing a vignette. The topic of the writing activity is business. First, the student is given some well-known sayings that contain the word business, and then, after you explain what one of the expressions means, he or she is asked to write a vignette that includes the saying.

Creative Thinking Skill to Be Developed: Being Original

Originality is a controversial term in the discussions of the people who write about creativity. Many still claim that true creativity occurs not only when someone does something new to society but when the product is significant to society. Others think of originality as being a god-given gift to humankind; it is the individual's privilege—and blessing—to express his or her individuality by interacting with the world in ways that are unique to him- or herself. The spirit of this unit is very close to the latter school of thought.

What comes out of this activity may not be terribly important, but it has a good chance of developing the student's ability to express him- or herself in an original way. The reason is that the student picks the expression that most interests him or her and then spins a small tale about how that expression came to be uttered. No one should choose the expression for the student, and so he or she must go ahead with the idea and develop it on his or her own.

Preparing for the Unit

Since the heart of the writing activity is dialogue, you may use this unit either to introduce that topic or to extend it. Dialogue provides vitality to stories, and, in this case, it is the heart of the little story to be written.

It may or may not be helpful to lead in to the unit with a remark or two about business. Perhaps the unit will work better if there is a tie-in to a discussion of business practices (always in the news), international business problems, or the plight of the downtown merchants as shopping centers increasingly move out of the city.

Presenting the Unit and Following Through with the Unit

The central issue in presenting this unit is whether or not you should do any of it orally. There is an opportunity to have a class discussion with the first part, which is concerned with the various expressions containing the word business. Then, however, the student is asked to explain one of those sayings, and so it would appear that a discussion of the expression would determine, to some extent, the student's interpretation of any of the sayings. You might discuss the sayings briefly and then ask if anyone knows of other expressions that feature the word.

This unit offers an excellent opportunity to have your students follow up their vignettes with more writing. They can either expand their vignette into a longer and more developed story, or they can write other vignettes. Since the vignette is brief, it has the appeal of being handled in a shorter period of time, with less of the agonizing that often goes with writing longer stories.

43 Business

1. In our society we have a number of sayings about business, possibly because, like most societies, business is very important in thescheme of things.

   Business is business.
   It's none of your business!
   What business is it of yours?
   No funny business, now!
   There's no business like show business.
   It's business as usual.

2. Choose one of these statements.

   Explain the statement, telling what it means in everyday discourse.

Business *(continued)*

3. Can you imagine a scene in which someone used exactly the expression you explained? Why might he or she be saying it? What might that person be like? To whom would he or she be saying it? What is the setting for this dialogue?

Write up the scene, telling what led to the remark about business and what happened afterward. See if you can inject some humor into this vignette.

44
Goofs

An Invitation to Invent Elaborate Alibis

Overview

The unit is comprised of an introductory section about mistakes and alibiing, an invitation to make up elaborate excuses for three mistakes having embarrassing legal and social ramifications, and an opportunity to think about what steps might have prevented the three mistakes. All three of the goofs are examples of what can happen to ordinary people who aren't prudent or circumspect in their actions—in other words, most of us who are sometimes preoccupied or confused.

Creative Thinking Skill to Be Developed: Being Original

This unit has its basis in the feeling all of us have when we say to ourselves, "I wish I hadn't done that (or had done this)!" Once a mistake is made, it can rarely be undone, however. The unit is also inspired by the "Alibi Ikes" of this world. Those people (young and old) have great imaginations, and they can think quickly, if deviously, on their feet or seat. Since they are simply making up stories, as we invite your students to do in this unit, the skill involved is one of inventing plots on the spot.

Preparing for the Unit

We fully expect that a majority of your students will identify with the incidents in this unit. Being young means making mistakes (not that being older means not making mistakes), and so students can probably remember a few recent goofs quite vividly.

It is generally true that as we grow older we tend to bury some of our negative experiences, but very embarrassing ones seem to surface all too often. A natural time to introduce this unit is after you, your principal, a secretary, or a custodian has goofed. (We'd guess that it would be least likely to have been the secretary.) Of all these candidates, the best example to cite would be you. It might be tempting to point out a student's goof, saying we all make mistakes, but no one—especially a preadolescent or an adolescent—wants attention given to his or her mistakes.

Presenting the Unit

The less serious part of this unit is the second section, in which your students contrive outlandish stories to "alibi out of" three embarrassing goofs. We hope they will give their imaginations free rein and invent some whoppers.

The more serious part comes at the end when we ask how these mistakes could have been avoided. The first two incidents are easy to prevent, and so your students should come up with the logical precautions that a fire setter should take and the use of a calendar that most people find so necessary in organizing their lives. Although mixing up names, as happens in the third incident, is not something you can anticipate accurately, associating names with faces and personalities and mentally preparing for introducing people are a couple of things all of us can do. Supposedly, it just takes mental effort and practice.

44 Goofs

1. The not-so-comforting saying "No one is perfect" is often heard when someone is trying to excuse someone else for a mistake or fault. It really isn't much consolation to the guilty party, however, to hear that everyone makes mistakes or has faults when the person knows some precaution or care would have prevented an error. We are more likely to find refuge in an alibi than to admit that we make mistakes, as everyone does.

There have been some very imaginative excuses offered for obvious goofs. People can be quite inventive when they are asked to explain a disastrous deed: they can link people, events, mechanisms, and forces in ways marvelous to hear. Are you good at alibiing? Here are some rather common mistakes. If you happen to have been guilty of them and wanted to shift responsibility away from yourself, what excuses would you give?

- You start a fire in an empty oil drum in the backyard to burn some papers and trash. A flaming paper escapes and sets fire to the dry weeds in the vacant lot next door. Since it is July and the weather has been hot and dry, the fire quickly spreads, and the fire department is called by a neighbor. When the fire crew arrives, they want to know what happened. What is your excuse?

- You arrive late to a party. At least you think that you are late. When you ring the doorbell of your host's house, however, he greets you with a very surprised look on his face. He says that you aren't expected until tomorrow evening, the time for which the party was scheduled. Very embarrassed, you try to think fast in order to come up with a plausible excuse for coming twenty-four hours early.

- You are at a party with a number of people of various ages. A group of five people find themselves together, and you are the only one who knows everybody in the group. So you introduce a young woman to another young woman. Unfortunately, because you get people's faces confused at times, you give the first young woman someone else's name. She, of course, corrects you, and you apologize quickly. You want to rescue some of your dignity and pride, however, and so you try to think of an explanation. What will you say?

2. As you know, the best policy in situations such as those given is to admit your guilt and be as honest as your deflated ego will allow you to be. But some people have a very difficult time admitting that they are wrong. Let's suppose that you are ten years older than you are now. You have learned the wisdom of planning and taking precautions. What would you do to avoid having those three embarrassing experiences?

Starting the brush fire

Arriving a day early for a party

Introducing someone and giving a wrong name

45
Just Three Questions

An Invitation to Write a Short Story

Overview

"Just Three Questions" begins with a brief introduction about the importance for an interviewer to ask intelligent questions. Then your students are asked to compose three thoughtful questions for five individuals who might be interviewed because of their exploits. That activity leads into the writing exercise, an invitation to write a short story in which one of the characters asks a question that determines the outcome of the story.

Creative Thinking Skill to Be Developed: Being Original

At this writing, talk shows on television and radio are as popular, or more popular, than ever. The craze doesn't go away. Therefore, the kind of preparation that an interviewer does before going on the air should seem a logical process to your students, whether or not any of them have an intention of playing such a role in the future. Perhaps most of them have even given some thought to the kinds of questions that they would like to hear asked. The point of the activity is, however, that the questions should not be predictable or hackneyed. Encourage your students to think of penetrating and searching questions.

Preparing for the Unit

Young people are naturally full of questions, but they do not always ask the kinds of questions that will increase their understanding. If there are times when your students ask senseless questions, these occasions can be cues for you to introduce "Just Three Questions." Without singling out any one student for criticism, you can get your message over by asking your students to restrict themselves to only three questions that they would particularly like to ask interesting people. Additional opportunities may arise to introduce the unit in a natural manner if any of the events described in the warm-up activity actually take place. You can allude to the event, and then note the similarity to the unit.

Presenting the Unit

Since asking questions is the way young children gain much of their information, it is natural that children in the primary grades depend upon their teachers to supply them with many of the answers to their questions. By the time they have reached the sixth grade, however, young people are not so convinced of their teachers' omniscience, and during the previous three or four years they have acquired a number of inhibitions that prevent their asking questions that need to be asked. Nevertheless, even such sophisticated individuals as middle school students and high school students frequently ask questions, and you still rate as an authority about certain subjects, despite the fact that you are not the all-knowing person your teaching counterpart in the elementary grades is.

This unit gives the student a chance to sharpen his or her skills as an interrogator without having to worry about being embarrassed in front of others. In the event the class finds any or all of the persons to be interrogated in the warm-up activity uninteresting, ask them to think of more promising subjects. In contradistinction to games such as "Twenty Questions," this unit invites the student to ask questions that do not lead to a single answer. The questions asked should be open-ended, questions that reflect what interests the student most about five remarkable people. If your students share their responses with you, the questions they ask should prove very revealing.

Following through with the Unit

After your students have competed the warm-up activity, an effective way of helping them learn from the experience is to ask the class to think about the reasons some questions are more effective in interviews than are others. If your students are interested, you might have them role-play one of the situations described in the unit. One student can play the part of the remarkable person, and another student who expresses special interest in this celebrity might pose to the first student the three questions he or she has formulated. After a number of these little episodes has been enacted, the class should be able to generalize about the art of question making and come up with some pertinent suggestions for making their questions more fruitful in the future.

45 Just Three Questions

1. If we know what questions to ask and how to ask them, we can gain much valuable information. In this unit you are to imagine that you are twenty-five years old and have landed a job as host on a television talk show. Your principal job is to ask questions of interesting people, questions that will provide your audience with useful and illuminating information. There is time on your program for just three questions for each of the persons to be interviewed. What questions would you ask the following individuals?

A chemist whose experiments have yielded an alloy that is lighter than aluminum, stronger than steel, and cheaper to produce than either aluminum or steel.

1. ______________________________

____

2. ______________________________

____

3. ______________________________

____

A twenty-year-old Peruvian poet who has just received a Nobel Prize for literature.

1. ______________________________

____

2. ______________________________

____

3. ______________________________

____

Just Three Questions *(continued)*

A professional bridge player who, with her partner, has just lost the world championship.

1. ______________________________

____

2. ______________________________

____

3. ______________________________

____

A fifteen-year old girl who surprised a burglar in her home one afternoon, managed to get a hammer lock on him with one hand and phone the police with the other, and then held him fast until the police arrived ten minutes later.

1. ______________________________

____

2. ______________________________

____

3. ______________________________

____

A man who returned a check from his bank within twenty minutes after he had discovered the bank had mistakenly made out the check for $22,560,000 instead of $22.56.

1. ______________________________

____

Just Three Questions *(continued)*

2. ____

____

3. ____

____

2. Why don't you write a short story in which one of the characters asks a question that determines the outcome of the action? You probably will want to write a mystery story or an adventure story, but it may be any kind of story that features a key question.

46 Civic Responsibilities

An Invitation to Write an Anecdote about Irresponsibility in a Future Community

Overview

This unit presents your students with a hypothetical problem in a community of the future. The community requires that its citizens, young and old, take care of public properties and services. But what happens when the goldbricks and goof-offs don't do their share of the work? Your students are asked to write about an incident in which one malingering citizen is taken to task for not assuming his or her share of the load.

Creative Thinking Skills to Be Developed: Producing Alternatives; Being Original

There probably will be considerable divergence in the ways in which your students solve the problem of how to deal with a recalcitrant citizen in the highly democratic community. It is always interesting to listen to young people talk about how we should deal with individuals who are guilty of transgressions. Some are quite harsh in their recommended punishments. Others are surprisingly wise.

As we say in the unit, there always will be people who lean on their oars. Encourage your students to reflect a good deal before using their imaginations in solving this ever-present problem. Tell them that they should think through the problem, listing a number of alternative solutions for correcting the situation. The tendency for most young people is to seize upon one solution and stick with it. Any possible action will have its advantages and disadvantages. Students should list those advantages and disadvantages, weighing them and thinking of the consequences for each.

Preparing for and Presenting the Unit

This unit can be utilized equally well in both social studies and language arts curricula. Any time a study of local government and the attendant problems of local and state governments are being undertaken is an excellent time to use "Civic Responsibilities." Our story was inspired by a little town in California that went broke and did use the local citizens to perform all of the jobs that were formerly paid for by taxes. Refusing to go any further in debt and not wishing to raise taxes, the mayor and her staff became volunteers. Many civic leaders followed suit, and the town got back on its financial feet.

The Writing Assignment

After thinking through the problem and listing possible solutions (with advantages and disadvantages), your students can then compose an anecdote in which the irresponsible citizen is dealt with in a proper way. There should be a little—not a lot—of background information about the community at the beginning of the anecdote in order to set the stage properly for the action. Similarly, the characters should be fleshed out to some extent in order that a reader can appreciate what forces are at work in this little drama.

46 Civic Responsibilities

1. This concerns someone your age who is living in a special place twenty years from now. Many features of that person's life are just about the same as they are in yours, but there are a few differences. For one thing, that young person has a full-time job but also attends a school. The school and the job are integrated; instructional sessions for basic skills and life skills are scheduled during each workday.

2. Another difference is the way in which people take care of the community. Everyone ten years old and older has a responsibility for the cleanliness, beauty, and safety of the community—without pay. There are people who don't do their part, of course, just as there always have been. In this community, everyone has a say in how things are done. What would happen in such a democratically oriented community when a person continually avoids his or her responsibilities? Do you think he or she would be publicly reprimanded, punished with extra duties, fined, ignored, or dealt with in some other way?

Civic Responsibilities *(continued)*

Write a hypothetical anecdote about an incident in which someone who is habitually negligent in carrying out his or her civic responsibilities is taken to task. Use the space below to formulate possible actions by the authorities.

47
Find the Missing Facts

An Invitation to Write a Mystery Story

Overview

This unit consists of three short anecdotes, each of which has facts missing that would explain its ending, and an invitation to write a mystery story. The anecdotes are set in undetermined times in the future, and therefore your students may be influenced by that feature.

Creative Thinking Skills to Be Developed: Seeing Relationships; Being Sensitive and Aware; Being Original

We can be sensitive to the phenomena of nature or to the moods of others. We can also be alert to trends and anticipate future events. For this unit, your students are encouraged to be aware of and look for missing elements. The elements of the warm-up activity are facts. Students are to search for the unstated facts, and those facts must relate to other facts in relationships that are logical and significant. We are hoping that after solving the little mysteries in the warm-up your students will want to invent an original mystery of their own. Incidentally, we have no preferred solutions to the three mysteries.

Preparing for the Unit

Some classes are more fond of solving puzzles than others. However, judging from the number of crossword puzzle and mystery story fans in our country, the chances are good that you have several students who like to solve puzzles. "Find the Missing Facts" can be introduced on almost any occasion when you are looking for a change of pace from the more routine tasks in your program. If your students have been doing any hypothesizing about why an event has taken place, or if they have been perplexed by someone's behavior (perhaps *your own,* if you would really like to set the stage for the activity), the unit can be brought in naturally and effectively.

Presenting the Unit

The idea of the warm-up activity is to cause your students to do some detective work. Their sleuthing will be mainly concerned with formulating hypotheses on the basis of the limited number of facts given in the anecdotes. Because there are only a few facts given in each situation, the student is able to allow his or her imagination to range freely. If some of the ideas produced by your students appear to be foolish or far-fetched but honestly conceived, give them respect. One of the greatest inhibitors of creative thinking is the fear of being ridiculed.

The writing assignment itself can be adapted and modified to suit whatever purposes you may have in using the unit. Since young people are apt to enjoy writing mystery stories, that particular form was chosen. However, there is nothing sacred about any part of this unit or any of the others in this book.

Following through with the Unit

Inasmuch as your students will probably be writing mystery stories as an outcome of the warm-up activity, you might read their productions and then pick one or two of the more suspenseful ones and have them read to the class. If you and your students think it a good idea, the reader might stop before the mystery is solved and ask the class for ideas about how it ends. This will give your students more practice in hypothesis making, an important part of the creative process. When the unit is completed, you should have several opportunities to notice whether your students have become more skillful in exploring possibilities and seeing causal relationships. You might also use this unit to make your students more aware of causal relationships in their own behavior.

47 Find the Missing Facts

1. This is an activity that requires you to use your imagination in trying to figure out why a certain event has taken place. Important facts have been left out of each of the anecdotes that follow. Your job is to come up with facts that will account for things turning out as they do. All of the events take place in the future.

   - Mary went to town one Saturday to do some shopping. Being a sentimental person, Mary decided to go to the last remaining department store in the downtown area of her city. She got off the bus at a busy corner and walked into the department store. Mary decided to take an elevator to the second floor and look at some hats. After trying on several hats, she started for an elevator whose doors were just opening. When Mary was about to step into the elevator, a man's voice echoed throughout the floor. It shouted, "Stop!" She fell to the floor.

     What facts have been omitted in this anecdote that would explain what happened?

   - Jerry drove his car to the lake one day when he felt like going swimming. It was the only lake within the county that wasn't polluted. Every other lake had "No Swimming!" signs posted, and people were fined if they were caught swimming in them. He parked his car by the side of the lake, got out, and jumped right into the water. After about ten minutes Jerry came out of the water. Just as he reached into his car for a towel, a police officer told him he was under arrest.

Find the Missing Facts *(continued)*

Think of as many facts as you can that might have been left out of this little story that would account for the police officer's action.

- Natasha came home early from her job in a genetic engineering laboratory because the neighbors had phoned her at work and complained about her dog's howling. It was all right to leave early because she had built up extra vacation/leisure hours by volunteering in her community's flood watch program. The business for which she worked gave credit to all of its employees for community service, and, because of the danger to the port city from tidal flooding, Natasha thought she could serve best in that way.

  Natasha and her dog went out for a walk, following a pathway leading through a park. It was a lovely spring day. Two birds twittered in an apple tree. A breeze stirred the branches of the tree, and several blossoms fell to the ground. Suddenly a rabbit darted across the path in front of Natasha and her dog. Without pausing, she and her dog proceeded down the path.

  Why didn't Natasha's dog chase the rabbit? What are some of the important facts that might have been omitted from this anecdote that would explain the dog's behavior?

Find the Missing Facts *(continued)*

2. If you enjoyed the detective work you did for the little stories above, you might like to write your own mystery story. Why don't you do some thinking about a plot that has a puzzle or a mystery that isn't revealed until the end of the story? Try to be as original as you can in developing your ideas, and remember that the essential element of a mystery story is suspense.

   Write your mystery in the space below.

48
Shortcuts

An Invitation to Write a Letter to the Editor

Preparing for the Unit

As is the case with all of the units in *What Next?* the ideal time to present this exercise is when the topic to be considered surfaces in the curriculum or in a class discussion. In the case of "Shortcuts," that topic itself may not be brought up (at least by that name), but the subjects of advertising, drugs, popularity, divorce, convenience foods, computerized processing of information, reading, and dancing may very well be discussed in class. All of them are subject to shortcutting, at least according to advertisers, drug pushers, cybernetics experts, and others.

Presenting the Unit

This unit has four levels of student involvement instead of the usual three, the fourth being the writing assignment. At the first level, the student is asked to name shortcuts for a variety of goals, from getting to school to gaining popularity and wealth. There may not be genuine shortcuts to achieving all of the twelve goals listed, but every day you can find people advertising shortcuts for every one of them except getting to school! If your students respond negatively to the question of whether any of these shortcuts are supposedly being made available, they aren't reading newspapers, magazines, or watching television. But, if your students say there is no genuine shortcut to popularity, they may be absolutely correct.

The implications of shortcutting to euphoria, fame, popularity, and divorce are very far-reaching, and, as you know all too well, they are often proposed and advertised in our society. This section of the unit is worthy of sufficient time in which to explore some of the points that are significant to your students.

At the second level, the student is asked to generalize about shortcutting and its consequences as well as to consider the roles played by talent and opportunity in reaching an important goal.

The third level takes the student into the indefinite future with a question about what shortcuts can next be expected to be touted in the print and electronic media. Four areas of living are to be explored—personal appearance, convenience foods, storing and retrieving information, and conserving energy—because they are presently being subjected to shortcuts and probably will be in the future. You certainly can add to the list or substitute other areas that may be more relevant to your students' concerns and interests.

The Writing Assignment

The writing assignment is actually a project that will take weeks to complete. It just possibly could be a most enlightening learning experience for your students. As is the case with many worthwhile projects, there are no genuine shortcuts (!) for your students in completing the assignment. They will have to do a considerable amount of reading, and, more accurately, they will have to do a lot of searching.

We expect that there will be no scarcity of ads proclaiming various shortcuts because in the week before this was written one local newspaper carried advertising offering immediate wealth (by a beneficent "millionaire" who can afford a full-page ad in the Sunday supplement); exquisite slimness as the result of several crash diets and the magic of health spas, as well as the traditional conversion of weakling to muscular marvel by makers of equipment and different health spas; quick and inexpensive divorces; and fast and effective ways to kick the tobacco habit.

Looking up the pertinent laws regulating advertising will require that your students find documents at the police department, post office and other government agencies, and at libraries and newspaper offices. The electronic retrieval systems offered in some of the larger libraries will be of immense benefit to your students if they have access to the systems. It would probably be a good idea for you to read the final draft of any letter sent to the newspaper editor, just in case the language used is a little rash or possibly libelous.

It might be helpful if you would have your entire class or group brainstorm possible sources of information about the problem they are researching. Here are some possible questions for use in brainstorming:

- What are the possible sources of printed information?
- What people might have expert information about the problem?
- What are some of the other nonprint sources of information about the problem?

After possible sources of information have been brainstormed, the possibilities should be evaluated by whatever criteria are important to the students. Here are some of the possible criteria:

- What will it probably cost?
- How much time will it probably take?
- How important is the information that this source might provide?

48 Shortcuts

1. Shortcuts are very appealing to many of us. We can't resist taking a shorter route if possible, even if it necessitates a little jaywalking or trespassing on occasion. Some of us are more inclined to take shortcuts than are others, but the practice is widespread—and growing. Shortcuts are touted continually in the media.

Do you know any shortcuts to

Getting to school? What are they?

Learning a new language? What are they?

Learning to draw well? What are they?

Getting a great physique? What are they?

Popularity? What are they?

Learning to dance well? What are they?

Writing a book? What are they?

Reading well? What are they?

Wealth? What are they?

Euphoria? What are they?

Shortcuts *(continued)*

Divorce? What are they?

Fame? What are they?

2. Answer the following questions in the spaces that follow.

Are there any genuine shortcuts for anything worthwhile, or do we always have to work hard to reach an important goal? Explain.

What about the factor of talent? How important is it?

How important is the factor of opportunity (or lack of it)?

3. Answer the following questions in the spaces that follow.

What shortcuts can we expect to be ballyhooed in the future? What can be expected in the field of personal appearance and grooming?

What advertising of shortcuts can be expected in the field of convenience foods?

What touting of shortcuts can be expected in the field of storing and retrieving information?

What can be expected in the way of advertising shortcuts in the field of conserving energy?

4. Some of the advertising that appears in newspapers borders on being fraudulent, and, of course, there have been many cases of misleading advertising in the print medium, some of which have been halted by the federal government. Why don't you look through five or six editions of your local newspaper to see if you can find an instance of misleading the public? If you find one, write a letter to the editor of the newspaper explaining how people are being misled and urging the paper not to accept the ad in the future. You'll need some facts to support your contentions, and so you will want to do research about the products or service being advertised. There are federal, state, and local laws forbidding fraudulent advertising, and you may want to become well informed about these.

You can jot down your findings about fraud laws in the space below.

49
Commonly Understood

An Invitation to Write a Set of Commonalities

Overview

This kind of activity is a familiar exercise in seeing relationships. It can also be used as a test. The activity itself, then, will look familiar to your students. There are two twists, however. The first is that the student is asked to substitute some other item for one of the three in each of the ten sets. The second is that the student is asked to compose his or her own exercise, but all of the items must deal with the future. Try it yourself. It is not very easy to do. Accordingly, you may have to allow quite a bit of time for the student to complete this unit. As a matter of fact, as with all the units in this book, the student should feel no pressure to complete the unit in a prescribed amount of time.

Creative Thinking Skill to Be Developed: Seeing Relationships

The ability to see relationships is basic to all thinking, but it is crucial in creative thinking. Of course, categorizing is the way in which we make sense of the world. The ability to see cause and effect is important not only when a baby touches something that is very hot but when an astronomer hypothesizes about puzzling phenomena universes away. Similarly, the ability to see commonalities in things is a key to the success of politicians, plumbers, accountants, detectives, teachers, writers, automobile mechanics, or anyone else who has to tackle problems and deal with people.

Preparing for the Unit

The major point we can make about your preparing for "Commonly Understood" is that you should make sure your students know that there isn't just one right answer to each of the sets. They should get the idea from the example at the beginning, which has more than one answer, that more than one acceptable answer exist; if there is any doubt about that point reinforce the fact that all ten of the sets of items have many commonalities.

There probably is no need for you to lead in to the unit except to convince your students that the activity is not a test. It can be administered at any time of the day or year, but preferably not after an examination.

Presenting the Unit

For the great majority of your students, responding to the ten sets of items should be quite easy. To the more reflective or unorthodox thinker there is an opportunity in this unit to think of unusual relationships. Accordingly, this activity should be a popular one for students who enjoy thinking differently from their classmates.

The third section of the unit invites the student to produce five sets of items with commonalities, all of which deal with the future. If you do attempt this part of the activity yourself, you will learn that it is challenging. Some students may not be able to come up with more than one or two items, and that, of course, is all right. The thing to watch for in administering creative thinking activities is frustration on the part of those students who are so used to memory and convergent thinking questions that they don't know how to react to open-ended questions and rely upon their own resources. It takes time for some of those students to learn to think divergently.

49 Commonly Understood

1. If you were to see these three items,
razor
dentist's drill
computer
what would you think they had in common? Pain? Machinery (if the razor is electric)? What else? ______________________________

Each item in the groups of words that follow has something in common with the other two items. When you have discovered what the three things have in common, write down your answer next to the three words.

1. pond, mirror, store window

2. radio, television, magazine

3. rye, wheat, rice

4. tea cup, envelope, shoe

5. tears, perspiration, red face

6. promotion, trophy, blue ribbon

7. thorax, abdomen, wings

8. door, mouth, book

9. firefly, North Star, kerosene lamp

10. nine, twenty-one, seventeen

2.

Now substitute a new item for one of the three items in each set of relationships.

Can you do it for every set and have the relationship you named remain the same?

1. ______________________________
____
2. ______________________________
____
3. ______________________________
____
4. ______________________________
____
5. ______________________________
____
6. ______________________________
____
7. ______________________________
____
8. ______________________________
____
9. ______________________________
____
10. ______________________________
____

Commonly Understood *(continued)*

3. Can you come up with five different sets of three items that have something in common but also deal with the future? Here is an example: log exports, overgrazing, drift nets

The commonality would be that regulation will be needed for each of these practices in the future.

See if you can produce five sets of items that deal with the future but are also linked in some way. Explain the relationships.

1. ______________________________
____
____
____

2. ______________________________
____
____
____

3. ______________________________
____
____
____

4. ______________________________
____
____
____

5. ______________________________
____
____
____

50
Squeaky Clean

An Invitation to Write Science Fiction

Overview

This unit explores a number of ways to use the expression "squeaky clean" and then invites your students to incorporate the term in a science fiction story about colonizing a planet. They may see no connection between "squeaky clean" and colonizing a planet, and, of course, there isn't any obvious direct relationship. We can hope that your students will stretch their minds and find a spot for the expression while tackling the central task of writing a story.

Creative Thinking Skills to Be Developed: Seeing Relationships; Being Original

In looking for ways of applying "squeaky clean" to ten highly diverse individuals, your students will be given considerable practice in seeing relationships. The theories concerning practice and skill are hoary ones in educational psychology. There are many factors involved in any attempt to increase skill through practice, and it often happens that the extraneous factors significantly affect the individual's performance in subsequent attempts to demonstrate a higher level of skill. It can be argued that the practice provided an individual student in completing this activity is too limited to result in greater skill at its conclusion. We agree with that argument, but we also know that certain experiences do open up individuals to possibilities they had not considered previously. This unit is a small sample of the opening-up experiences that young people can have in learning to express their distinctive personalities.

Preparing for the Unit

Expressions such as "squeaky clean" are very common in our version of the English language. Some are quite picturesque; others are trite and after a while grate on the ear. A discussion of slang, metaphors, similes, tired expressions, or the automatic phrases that serve as social conventions could lead into this unit or follow it. Since the unit culminates in a writing activity, you may prefer to lead in with a discussion of a current "buzzword" or trite expression that is prominent in the language of your students.

Presenting the Unit

For most students, there isn't anything terribly difficult about applying "squeaky clean" to the U.S. senator, household worker, and the other eight people listed in the activity. All ten want to be very clean—or at least perceived as such—in their jobs. We can assume, then, that this part of the unit is a rather painless warm-up for the writing exercise. If any of your students balk at being asked to write about colonizing a planet, you can either substitute another topic or divert their energies in another direction. It might be effective if you reinforce our challenge and comment that it will be most interesting to see how that old expression can be inserted in a story about future interplanetary exploration.

50 Squeaky Clean

1. There once was a television ad for a shampoo that proclaimed your hair would be "squeaky clean" after using that product. That term has been used also to describe people who are above reproach in their honesty. Ralph Nader, who crusades against corruption in the business and government worlds, has been so described. The term might also be applied, quite literally, to things such as kitchen floors, windows, table tops, chalkboards, and car hoods. It is a term that can be used in many other contexts, too.

If you were a writer of short stories or novels, you might use "squeaky clean" for the following characters. If you did, what would you be trying to convey?

a household servant

a hospital nurse

a person accused of a theft

a criminal lawyer

a college basketball player

an agent who represents college athletes who want to become professional players

a U.S. Senator

a newspaper columnist who writes about politics

Squeaky Clean *(continued)*

a dentist

a reformed addict

2. If you were a science fiction writer and were writing about the colonization of a planet, in what situation in your story would you use the term "squeaky clean"?

   Outline your science-fiction plot in the space below.

51
Twenty More Years

An Invitation to Write a Narrative

Overview

The next-to-last unit in this collection of ideas for thinking creatively about the future is meant to concern the individual student about his or her future. It can be summed up in one question: "What are you going to do with your life?" Will it be a round of parties and a life dedicated to the pursuit of pleasure? Will it be a life of purpose, dedicated to rewards and glory? Or will it be a life of aimlessness? From the sixth grade on, we encourage our students to start thinking about their futures. This unit tries to do just that in a rather straightforward manner.

Creative Thinking Skill to Be Developed: Anticipating Consequences

The skill to be developed in this unit is of utmost importance to all of us, that is, anticipating the consequences of our behavior. Although experience is a great teacher, we are not always good students.

Preparing for and Presenting the Unit

Because this is a serious unit, it should be administered at a time when your students are receptive to the idea of taking a good look at their futures. We didn't attempt to inject humor into this unit, in contrast with most of the other units in *What Next?* Accordingly, your students shouldn't be in a particularly frivolous mood when you introduce "Twenty More Years." It might be possible for our questions to do their work if your students are in a carefree mood, but it would be best if you found a time when they are purposeful and task oriented.

The Writing Assignment

Five activities may be too many when it comes to showing their influence in a single day, so you may want to cut the number to two or three. Even one activity might be better. We chose five simply because the list of activities given is fairly long. Use your judgment in this regard. It is a challenge for most students to do this writing exercise conscientiously. It will require a good deal of imagination and also logical thinking to do it well.

51 Twenty More Years

1. Which of these activities do you engage in regularly? Underline them.

jogging
playing football
riding a bicycle
drawing, sketching, painting
driving a car
listening to the radio
dancing
playing card games
writing poetry
writing drama
writing letters
conversing with friends
repairing things

playing basketball
swimming
playing tennis
riding a horse
watching television
singing
playing video games
listening to music
going to parties
feeding and caring for animals
taking photographs
constructing things

weight training
playing baseball or softball
riding a motorcycle
reading for pleasure
meditating
going to movies
playing a musical instrument
giving parties
writing fiction (novels, short stories)
smoking or chewing tobacco
inventing things
gardening

Select the five activities you do most often and list them.

Twenty More Years *(continued)*

2. What will twenty years of doing these five activities mean to you and do to you? For example, what will twenty years of smoking, watching television, playing a musical instrument, playing video games, and going to parties mean to you at the end of those twenty years? How will those experiences change you?

Write about what one day of your life will be like as a result of those twenty years of engaging in your five favorite activities.

52 Finished?

An Invitation to Make Predictions about the Future

Overview

After an introduction pertaining to the psychological need for closure we humans have, we ask your students to predict whether or not they will attain five goals that nearly anyone would describe as necessary for a fulfilled life. Your students are then taken from a personal perspective to the broader one of predicting how well the American people will do in striving for seven highly desirable societal goals.

Creative Thinking Skill to Be Developed: Being Sensitive and Aware

Your students are asked to do a good deal of forecasting for this unit. If they attempt to be quasi-scientific, they can make their predictions in the form of hypotheses. The creative thinking skill that we hope to develop in this unit is being sensitive to and aware of problems. That development won't occur, however, unless your students dig in and do some thinking, discussing, and researching. Merely tossing out opinions vaguely held or borrowed from others won't permit your students to gain very much by engaging in this activity. They should spend some time trying to get at the factors involved in the issues.

Preparing for the Unit

This unit "covers the waterfront." There is hardly a day of the school year that the unit can't be tied in with topics in the curriculum and from world affairs. You can try to select a time when one of the personal goals listed has been touched upon (for example, financial security or family relationships) as appropriate for administering the unit. Our strategy is to take your students from their personal concerns to societal and global issues.

Presenting the Unit

It may strike you that there is "too much" in this unit because it brings up most of the major goals an individual in our society is confronted with at present. Not only could the unit take up two or three class sessions, but it could occupy your students for weeks. Therefore, you can guide your students according to the limitations they have in terms of time and resources. It is possible to administer the unit in one class period and follow it up with a discussion in the next. Unfortunately, brief responses mean less thinking and learning.

Of course, you might find that the themes in this unit have been sounded so often that your students aren't fully motivated to respond to them. A good deal will depend upon how seriously they regard the activity of *predicting* how well they and American society can meet the challenges ahead.

52 Finished?

1. Franz Schubert wrote only two movements of his eighth symphony. Ever since the symphony was first played, it has been known as the "Unfinished Symphony." Other composers have failed to complete symphonies, but Schubert's is the one known as unfinished.

The idea of leaving something incomplete is somewhat troublesome to most of us, although there are people who continually leave projects unfinished. To the majority of us, though, there is a feeling of definite discomfort when a task is not completed. Psychologists call this urge the "need for closure." When viewed broadly, we can talk of finishing one's work in life. "His life's work was done when he finally finished the third book of his trilogy at the age of eighty-eight" might be the statement of a biographer. In a sense, however, no life can ever be truly complete because there are always goals one can accomplish, regardless of the individual's age. Which of these goals can you attain in your lifetime? Tell why you think they will or will not be reached.

A body largely free of serious illness.

Permanent and loving relationships with members of your family.

Finished? *(continued)*

Employment that is challenging and fulfilling.

Development of your talents to an extent that they allow you to express yourself well and also gain some measure of recognition from others.

Spirituality that steadily grows during your lifetime.

2. Every society has its goals, too. Some of the obvious goals of society are often part of a presidential candidate's campaign rhetoric. Tell why each of these goals can either succeed or fail in your lifetime.

A reduction in crime in the cities to the extent that jails and prisons are not only uncrowded but actually half empty.

A health care plan for all citizens of the United States.

A genuine cure for AIDS that is available and free to anyone.

A great reduction in the rate of pregnancies of unwed teenagers.

An automobile that is not fueled by gasoline and is used by a majority of motorists.

Finished? *(continued)*

No additional species added to the list of endangered species in the United States because of the efforts of the great majority of citizens to protect wildlife.

The cessation of the devastation of forests throughout the Western Hemisphere.